This publication was made possible by the kind support of

Binational Softwood Lumber Council – www.softwoodlumber.org
Cree – www.creebyrhomberg.com
Forest and Wood Products Australia – www.fwpa.com.au
Forestry Innovation Investment – www.bcfii.ca
reThink Wood Initiative – www.rethinkwood.com

TALL WOOD BUILDINGS
DESIGN, CONSTRUCTION AND PERFORMANCE

MICHAEL GREEN
JIM TAGGART

Birkhäuser

Basel

Layout, cover design and typography Miriam Bussmann, Berlin
Editor Ria Stein, Berlin
Production Katja Jaeger, Berlin
Project management for MGA | Michael Green Achitecture
Stuart Lodge, Vancouver
Paper 135g/m² Hello Fat matt 1.1
Printing Grafisches Centrum Cuno GmbH & Co. KG, Calbe
Cover Wood Innovation and Design Centre, Prince George, Canada
Cover photograph Ed White, Vancouver

Library of Congress Cataloging-in-Publication data
A CIP catalog record for this book has been applied for at the Library of Congress.
Bibliographic information published by the German National Library
The German National Library lists this publication in the Deutsche Nationalbibliografie;
detailed bibliographic data are available on the Internet at http://dnb.dnb.de.

This publication is also available as an e-book (ISBN PDF 978-3-0356-0476-4;
ISBN EPUB 978-3-0356-0481-8) and in a German language edition
(ISBN 978-3-0356-0474-0).

© 2017 Birkhäuser Verlag GmbH, Basel
P.O. Box 44, 4009 Basel, Switzerland
Part of Walter de Gruyter GmbH, Berlin/Boston

Printed on acid-free paper produced from chlorine-free pulp. TCF ∞

Printed in Germany

ISBN 978-3-0356-0475-7

9 8 7 6 5 4 3 2 1
www.birkhauser.com

CONTENTS

FOREWORD

We are living in an age which will come to be dominated by our relationship with the planet. As the changes to our climate become ever more apparent, the way we live and inhabit the earth will, by necessity, be transformed.

A fundamental change in the way in which we build our cities is imperative, re-learning how to build in timber and how to build tall with the new engineered timbers that the 21st century technologies allow will be fundamental to our future. This new age of architecture takes us beyond the notions of modernism and concrete construction to a new timber age.

Timber is the only construction material that can be grown and as it grows it consumes carbon. Using timber not only reduces our impact on the planet but will also help to reverse some of the effects of 20th century industrialization. Timber construction is not only healthy for our planet but is also healthy for humans. Living and working in timber buildings is good for the soul and good for health. The time has come again to leave behind inhospitable concrete caves and embrace the timber age.

A new architecture will emerge as we learn how to build in timber. We are the very beginning of this new and exciting era, this book marks the beginning of this new age and will help to provide the inspiration and momentum for the exciting new architecture to come.

Andrew Waugh
Waugh Thistleton Architects, London
August 2016

WOOD, A MATERIAL FOR OUR TIME

As the 21st century unfolds, architecture stands at a crossroads. Until now there has been no reason to challenge the supremacy of concrete and steel as the materials of choice for high-rise buildings, but in the past decade our evaluation criteria have become more complex. The core tenets of 'commodity, firmness and delight', first proposed by the Roman architect Vitruvius 2000 years ago as the prerequisites for a fine building, now fall within a framework of pressing global imperatives that are daunting in both scale and scope. The practice of architecture must now encompass the issues of climate change, population growth, and a global housing shortage.

In the spring of 2015, the National Oceanic and Atmospheric Administration (NOAA), a scientific agency based in Washington, DC, announced that changes in the Earth's climate system had reached a significant and disturbing milestone. For the first time since the NOAA began measuring the concentration of carbon dioxide in the atmosphere at 40 sites around the globe, the average of those monthly measurements exceeded 400 parts per million (ppm).

According to the NOAA, this represents an increase of approximately 120ppm since industrialization began about 200 years ago. As we know, the rapid rise in CO_2 emissions has been driven by technological development, population growth and the commensurate increase in fossil fuel consumption. However, the accumulation of CO_2 and other greenhouse gases in the atmosphere has not been linear, as 60ppm of the increase has occurred in the last 50 years, and 7.5ppm in the last three years alone.

At 400ppm, the atmospheric concentration of CO_2 is at a level not seen on Earth for millions of years and the implications are significant. In the words of Dr. Erika Podest, carbon and water cycle research scientist with NASA: 'This milestone is a wakeup call that our actions in response to climate change need to match the persistent rise in CO_2. Climate change is a threat to life on Earth and we can no longer afford to be spectators.'[1]

Implicit in Dr. Podest's statement is the assertion that we cannot manifest the changes that are necessary to stabilize the climate system simply by fine-tuning our current way of doing things – rather we must completely transform our commercial and industrial practices to radically reduce, and ultimately eliminate, their carbon footprint.

Also in the spring of 2015, two devastating earthquakes in Nepal, resulting in the collapse of hundreds of buildings and the loss of more than 8000 lives, came as a tragic reminder of the substandard conditions in which far too many people in the developing world live and work. As with climate change, the statistics are alarming. UN Habitat has estimated that 1 billion people (one in seven of the world's population) currently live in slums, and a further 100 million are homeless.[2]

As the world population continues to increase, it is projected that we will need to construct 3 billion units of affordable housing over the next 20 years. The vast majority of these will be required in the cities of the developing world, where population growth is taking place most rapidly.

At first glance the challenges of climate change and world housing might appear to be unrelated. Of the two, climate change receives more attention in the developed world, as its environmental and economic effects are felt directly in the wake of increasingly frequent hurricanes and floods, droughts and forest fires. By contrast, while access to adequate and secure housing is recognized by the United Nations as a universal human right, it is not a daily concern for most people in the West.

The reverse is true in the developing world, where vast numbers of people live at or below the poverty line, and for whom the overriding concern is the day to day search for enough food to eat and a safe place to sleep. Understandably, for those living in such circumstances, the mitigation of climate change may be so far beyond their control that it is nothing more than an abstract concept.

However, leaders in the sustainability movement increasingly believe that the solution to the environmental crisis is inextricably intertwined with issues of equity, democracy and social justice – not just within national boundaries, but across the world. This position was eloquently summarized by Andrew Ross in his 2011 book *Bird on Fire*, when he wrote: 'The task of averting drastic climate change might be described as an experiment – a vast social experiment in decision-making and democratic action. Success in that endeavour will not be determined primarily by large technological fixes, though many will be needed along the way. Just as decisive to the outcome is whether our social relationships, cultural beliefs, and political customs will allow for the kind of changes that are necessary. That is why the climate crisis is as much a social as a biophysical challenge, and why the solutions will have to be driven by a fuller quest for global justice than has hitherto been tolerated or imagined.'[3]

To frame the challenge in architectural terms, approximately one third of global greenhouse gas (GHG) emissions are attributable to the construction and operation of buildings. The Intergovernmental Panel on Climate Change (IPCC) has estimated that these emissions increased at an annual average of more than 2% between 1971 and 2004. Historically the majority of GHG emissions were generated by the highly developed countries of North America, Europe and Central Asia. However by 2030, it is projected that these emissions will be surpassed by those from developing countries, and overall emissions will be almost twice the 2004 levels.[4]

The production of our most widely used construction material, namely concrete, is already responsible for

between 5% and 8% of global GHG Greenhouse emissions. We produce approximately 3 tonnes of concrete per year for every person on the planet. Although this figure also includes concrete used in a variety of infrastructure applications, it nonetheless represents a significant proportion of the emissions attributable to the construction and operation of buildings. As for steel, while it is less carbon-intensive than concrete, and is relatively efficient to recycle, the production of steel accounts for about 4% of global energy use.[5]

To address the housing shortage, construction activity in the developing world will have to increase exponentially, yet our current materials and technologies cannot deliver this increased volume of construction without grave negative consequences for the environment. If we were to proceed with 'business as usual', the increase in construction activity would generate incalculable quantities of greenhouse gases, and a potentially catastrophic acceleration of climate change.

While reducing the operating energy required to heat and cool buildings is dependent on regionally based solutions that respond to the particularities of local climate, reducing the energy intensity of building construction can be achieved using a universal approach. The typologies of mid- and high-rise urban housing are essentially the same everywhere, and currently realized using a combination of load-bearing concrete masonry and concrete or steel frame systems. The only material we have available to us that could deliver housing solutions on the scale required – and at the same time reduce the GHG emissions associated with construction – is wood.

New massive wood products such as cross-laminated timber (CLT), together with computerized design and fabrication techniques, have accelerated the development of new approaches to building with wood. Calculations have indicated that some of these approaches may be applied to structures in excess of 40 storeys. Although research and development of these new approaches is concentrated in Europe and North America, the implications for the global construction industry are profound.

The expansion of wood construction at this scale must be predicated on the exclusive use of material harvested from independently certified, sustainably managed forests. Only third-party certification provides the necessary guarantee that the rate of wood harvest does not exceed the rate of forest regeneration, and will therefore not result in deforestation and further contribute to climate change.

The purpose of this book is to present the arguments in favour of 'Tall Wood' buildings and to showcase completed projects that demonstrate the applicability of this technology to construction across a wide range of building types, and in a variety of physical and cultural contexts.

While Tall Wood construction can only ever be part of the solution to the social and environmental challenges we face, its adoption around the world would represent the kind of transformational thinking and cooperative action that will be essential if we are to restore equilibrium to the world's climate system, and eliminate the inequities that have contributed to our current problems.

Michael Green and Jim Taggart
Vancouver, Canada
May 2016

REFERENCES

1 NASA (2014). *Global Climate Change – Vital Signs of the Planet.* Retrieved from 'NASA scientists react to 400 ppm carbon milestone'. http://climate.nasa.gov/400ppmquotes/

2 UN Habitat (2014). *World Habitat Day Background Paper.* Retrieved from http://unhabitat.org/wp-content/uploads/2014/07/WHD-2014-Background-Paper.pdf

3 Ross, A. (2011). *Bird on Fire: Lessons from the World's Least Sustainable City.* Oxford University Press.

4 United Nations Environmental Program (2013). *Buildings and Climate Change: Summary for Decision Makers.* Retrieved from http://capacity4dev.ec.europa.eu/unep/document/buildings-and-climate-change-summary-decision-makers

5 UN IPCC (2007). *Climate Change 2007 – Mitigation of Climate Change.* Retrieved from http://www.ipcc.ch/pdf/assessment-report/ar4/wg3/ar4_wg3_full_report.pdf

WOOD, SUSTAINABILITY AND CLIMATE CHANGE

At least in theory, wood is the ultimate sustainable building material. It is strong, durable, renewable and, above all, manufactured by the sun. In practice, however, what remains at issue, is whether we can manage our forest resources in a way that meets our needs without reducing their area, or compromising the ecological services they provide as reservoirs of carbon, purifiers of air and water, sanctuaries of biodiversity and providers of animal habitat.

These concerns are legitimate, as deforestation and its negative effects remain a significant problem in some regions of the developing world. While forest certification organizations continue to work with governments and industry in these areas to establish sustainable forest management (SFM) practices and protocols, these are already in place throughout the major wood-producing countries of the developed world. Thus the focus of this book is on those regions; continental Europe, Scandinavia, North America and Australasia.

FORESTS TODAY

As long ago as 2001, the United Nations Food and Agriculture Organization (UNFAO) determined that, in these regions at least, loss of forest cover is no longer a quantitative issue. In parts of Europe, the United States and Canada, the area of forests is actually increasing, with North America now approaching the level of forest cover it had when the first European settlers arrived in the early 17th century.[1]

The nature and make-up of contemporary forests varies significantly from country to country according to local climate, geographical latitude and elevation [ill. p. 14 top]. Forests that are regulated and managed for commercial wood production also vary greatly. In some jurisdictions, such as New Zealand, commercial timber for structural applications comes from plantation forests where a single exotic species, in this case Monterey or radiata pine (*Pinus radiata*), predominates, and native hardwood forests are set aside as reserves. In Tasmania, where growing conditions are very similar, long-established plantations of radiata pine are now being supplemented by stands of native eucalypts on an experimental basis.

In Northern Europe, forests are dominated by two indigenous species, Norway spruce (*Picea abies*) and Scots pine (*Pinus sylvestris*), although the forests also contain Central European varieties such as oak (*Quercus robur*) and beech (*Fagus sylvatica*). Central and Eastern Europe have significant areas of broadleaf (hardwood) forests. Approximately 70% of Europe's forest cover is semi-natural, having been modified to some degree by human intervention, yet retaining natural characteristics. Only 8% is plantation forest, found mainly in Denmark, the Netherlands, Portugal, Ireland and the United Kingdom.

In the boreal regions of Canada, black spruce (*Picea mariana*) and white spruce (*Picea glauca*) predominate, while on the west coast (and in the Pacific Northwest region of the United States) forests in wetter regions contain a mixture of Douglas fir (*Pseudotsuga menziesii*), western hemlock (*Tsuga heterophylla*) and western red cedar (*Thuja plicata*). In drier parts of the west coast, a combination of spruce, pine and fir species prevails.[2] In the southeastern United States, the naturally mixed forests consist of a variety of pine species, generally referred to collectively as 'southern yellow pine'.[3] Together, the forests of North America constitute 20% of the world's total.

To a greater or lesser degree, all healthy forests provide the kinds of ecological services mentioned above, and can continue to do so when commercial wood production is properly managed. Even the exotic plantation forests of New Zealand have an under-storey of native shrubs that support a greater degree of biodiversity than would be found in open prairie or agricultural land.

Some countries, such as Estonia and Scotland, are actively reforesting unproductive grassland, recognizing both the economic and environmental benefits this can bring. Overall, the regions that are the primary focus of this book have either stable or increasing areas of forest cover [ill. p. 14 bottom].

SUSTAINABLE FOREST MANAGEMENT

Despite the great variety of natural, semi-natural and plantation forest types, there are third-party administered, internationally recognized sustainable forest management (SFM) protocols applicable to each. These protocols provide assurance to governments, industry, architects and the public alike that the quantity of wood fibre harvested does not exceed the quantity of wood fibre produced by tree growth on an annual basis, nor compromises the ecological services the forest provides. Such protocols are well established in Scandinavia, Western and Central Europe and North America and the area of forests under SFM is increasing rapidly in Eastern Europe, Central America and Asia [ill. p. 15].

Regardless of forest type or jurisdiction, sustainable forest management is typically founded on the following core principles:

- Conserve biodiversity;
- Maintain the productive capacity of forest ecosystems;
- Maintain the vitality and health of forest ecosystems;
- Conserve and maintain soil and water resources;
- Maintain the forest contribution to global carbon cycles;
- Maintain and enhance long-term, multiple socioeconomic benefits to meet the needs of societies; and
- Provide legal, institutional and economic frameworks for forest conservation and sustainable management.

World map depicting overall forest cover

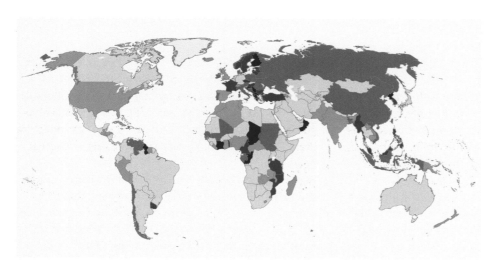

m³/hectare

<50	150–200
50–100	>200
100–150	no data

World map depicting percentage of land area dedicated to commercial forestry

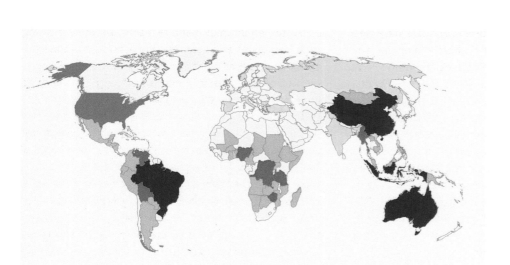

Net loss	Net gain
>500	250–500
250–500	50–250
50–250	>500

World map depicting annual decrease and increase in forest cover

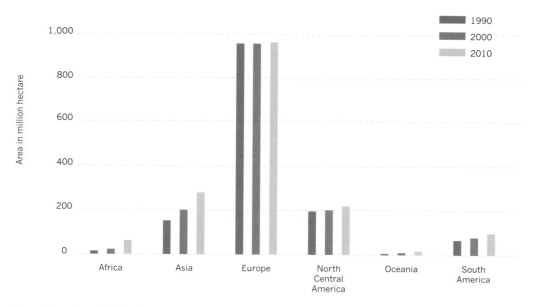

■ 1990
■ 2000
□ 2010

Area of forest certified under sustainable forest management by region

Third-Party Certification

Based on these principles, national and regional standards are developed in consultation with a variety of stakeholders to set parameters for the desired age and density of trees and composition of tree species within individual management areas; and the distribution of forest types and age classes (i.e. stands of trees of similar age) within a region.

Internationally, the efficacy and integrity of the majority of regional and national systems is endorsed by the Programme for the Endorsement of Forest Certification Schemes (PEFC). PEFC is a non-profit, non-governmental organization based in Geneva, Switzerland, that works throughout the entire forest supply chain to promote good forestry practices. Applying the core principles listed above, PEFC certification assures that timber and non-timber forest products have been produced with respect for the highest ecological, social and ethical standards. Forests certified under the umbrella of PEFC constitute approximately 65% of the world's certified forests.

Countries with PEFC-endorsed national certification systems include Australia, Austria, Canada, Finland, France, Germany, Italy, Norway, Sweden, Switzerland, the United Kingdom and the United States. The second-most popular forest certification system is administered by the Forest Stewardship Council (FSC). FSC is also a non-profit, multi-stakeholder organization that sets standards, certifies forests and administers a 'chain of custody' labelling program.

Increasingly, PEFC and FSC are seen by governments and industry as having very similar objectives and standards, although these are realized through different approaches. PEFC is a 'bottom up' organization, as it facilitates mutual recognition between nationally developed standards; whereas FSC is a 'top down' organization, developing its own standards and adapting them to a variety of regional bio-climates and forest types.

In the spring of 2016, the US Green Building Council, which had previously recognized only the FSC standard as eligible for credit under its Leadership in Energy and Environmental Design (LEED) rating system, extended that recognition to include PEFC.

THE ROLE OF FORESTS IN THE CARBON CYCLE

With SFM protocols firmly in place in most developed countries, what makes sustainable forest management of continued interest is the fact that, because growing trees sequester and store carbon dioxide and other greenhouse gases from the atmosphere, increasing the responsible use of wood can actually contribute to the long-term mitigation of climate change.

Historically, the composition of the Earth's atmosphere was held in balance in part by the ability of forests to absorb carbon dioxide and release oxygen. For most of its life, a growing tree uses the sunlight it receives to sequester CO_2 and convert the carbon it contains into cellulose, the main component of wood fibre [ill. p. 16]. This carbon remains in the wood until the tree begins to decay or is destroyed by fire, at which point it is released again as CO_2. This process is part of a complex system of global carbon exchange known as the carbon cycle.

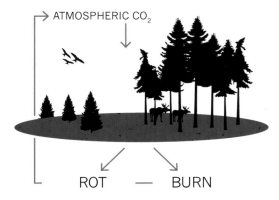

Carbon cycle for a natural forest

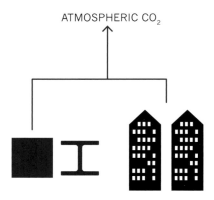

Carbon cycle for a managed forest yielding traditional solid sawn wood products

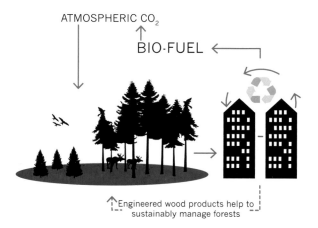

Carbon cycle for a managed forest yielding engineered wood products

However, the capacity of this system has been compromised by deforestation, population growth and by the increased per capita impact of human activity dependent on fossil fuel. This process has accelerated rapidly in the last 200 years and we are now entering a period of unprecedented climate instability.

Maintaining Forest Carbon Stocks

Forests and the soils that support them are a major component of the terrestrial biosphere, which, in turn, is one of the five reservoirs in the Earth's carbon storage and exchange system. Across the vast temperate and boreal forests, the proportions of total forest carbon stored in the trees and in the soil varies considerably. In temperate regions the average is believed to be around 65% in the soil and 35% in the vegetation, while in the boreal forests these figures may be as much as 80% in the soil and as little as 20% in the vegetation.

Left undisturbed, the most common mechanism of renewal in forests is fire (although disease, insect attack and windfall also play a part). While fire releases large amounts of carbon from the vegetation it burns, it leaves the carbon in the soil largely intact. By contrast, harvesting has little impact on the carbon in the vegetation, but can release large quantities of carbon from the soil it disturbs. This amount varies considerably with the harvesting method employed.

Over large areas, it is difficult to accurately estimate the volume of wood and other vegetation (and hence the total carbon stored) in a forest. Such calculations must rely on aerial photography and limited field measurements of tree sizes and spacing.

However, within smaller tracts of land where more comprehensive field measurements are achievable, or in plantation forests where tree size and spacing is consistent, it is possible to refine these calculations considerably. Sophisticated computer modelling tools enable forest regulators and forestry companies to compare the environmental impacts of different harvesting methods, and to ensure that (when all impacts and benefits are measured) these activities do

An analysis of the wood structure and finishes of the Eugene Kruger Building, Laval University, Gauthier Gallienne Moisan Architectes, 2005, in Quebec City, Canada demonstrated a significant reduction in embodied energy compared to a steel equivalent.

The imported solid wood structure of the Forte Building, designed by Andrew Nieland/Lend Lease Corporation and built in 2012 in Melbourne, Australia, has a lower carbon footprint than a similar structure built from local concrete.

not diminish overall forest carbon stocks or contribute to climate change.

Carbon Sequestration

In addition to measuring forest carbon stocks, sustainable forest management techniques can also enable us to optimize the relationship between forest growth and wood production. The rate at which trees absorb CO_2 varies with species, but in all cases is directly proportional to the rate of growth. Saplings and young trees grow very rapidly, but as trees mature their rate of growth slows, and consequently their rate of CO_2 absorption. In overmature trees CO_2 absorption stops altogether. When trees die and start to decay, they begin to release the CO_2 they contain. Without continuous regeneration, forests can actually become net emitters of CO_2.

SFM can optimize the carbon sequestration rate of forests through a managed process of harvesting and regeneration. For every climate, region and forest type, there is an optimal amount of harvest based on the annual growth rate. This annual increase in wood fibre volume is known as the stem wood increment. Over time, harvesting at a rate less than the stem wood increment will result in an overmature forest, just as surely as harvesting at a rate greater than the stem wood increment will ultimately result in deforestation. While ongoing monitoring through SFM protocols is required, there is a potential benefit to climate change mitigation if we harvest at a rate equal (or close) to the stem wood increment. By optimizing the volume of wood fibre harvested from our forests in this way, we can also optimize carbon sequestration.

CARBON STORAGE, WOOD SUBSTITUTION AND EMBODIED ENERGY

When we transform wood into building products or other durable items (although not pulp and paper), the benefits of carbon storage become longlasting. The carbon in the products made from harvested trees remains encapsulated, while the new trees planted in their place begin to bind new carbon, ensuring that

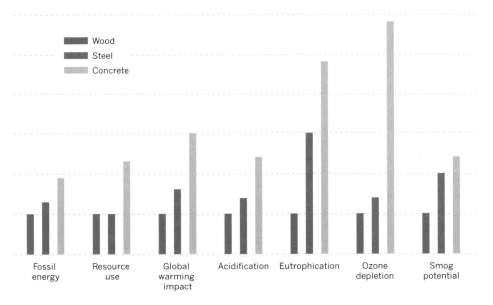

Wood
Steel
Concrete

Fossil energy | Resource use | Global warming impact | Acidification | Eutrophication | Ozone depletion | Smog potential

Comparison of life cycle environmental impact of buildings by primary construction material

the cycle continues. The amount of carbon stored in wood varies with tree species, but for most softwoods used in construction, the rate of storage is approximately 1 tonne of CO_2 per cubic metre.

The environmental benefits of wood are further enhanced when one takes into account that an increase in the use of wood results in a commensurate reduction in the use of other more carbon-intensive materials. Furthermore, the processing of harvested trees into sawn lumber or engineered wood products also takes considerably less input energy than that required to process other common construction materials such as steel and concrete [ill. p. 18 above].

When used in reference to building construction, the term 'embodied energy' means the amount of energy required to extract, process, fabricate, transport and install a particular material or product. The amount of embodied energy will be influenced by the energy intensity of the processes used for extraction and production, the distance that raw materials and fabricated components must travel, and the mode of transportation used. In regard to extraction and production processes, there is an assumed relationship between embodied energy and GHG emissions, although this will vary according to the source of energy used – whether hydro-electricity, coal or another fuel. Published data can be confusing, as comparisons of GHG emissions are sometimes presented by volume and sometimes by weight.

Materials such as wood, steel and concrete require different cross sections or dimensions to perform the same functions (whether beams or columns, floors or walls), so the most meaningful method for presenting data is in the form of a whole structure or whole building comparison. Embodied energy and related GHG emissions can then be calculated for identical buildings constructed in each material or combination of materials.

In the last ten years, analysis of wood structures, such as the structure and cladding of the Eugene Kruger Building in Quebec City, Canada [ill. p. 17 left] and many others since, have consistently demonstrated reductions in embodied energy and GHG emissions of 50–90% when compared to steel or concrete systems. One advantage for wood products is that many sawmills and manufacturing plants now generate their electricity using wood waste bio-fuel, which is a carbon-neutral energy source.

With respect to the embodied energy due to transportation, distance is only part of the equation. In the United Kingdom, which does not have sufficient locally grown timber, nor the infrastructure to manufacture massive wood products, cross-laminated timber panels fabricated in Germany and Austria and transported by road are calculated to have a lower carbon footprint (the sum of the GHG emissions related to embodied energy) than locally manufactured concrete. Similarly, and more surprisingly, Australia's Lend Lease Corporation determined that significant carbon savings are possible with massive timber even when procuring non-local materials. CLT imported from Austria was used in the construction of its Forte Building, a ten-storey apartment building on the Melbourne waterfront [ill. p. 17 right]. This is in part due to the carbon sequestered in the wood when compared to the carbon footprint of concrete or steel, and in part to the low embodied energy of shipping compared to road transportation. Completed in 2012, Forte also demonstrated that a structural wood solution could be cost-competitive in the Australian market when compared with more conventional building materials such as concrete or steel.

Life Cycle Assessment

Increasingly, the preferred method of comparison (and the most comprehensive to date) is that of life cycle assessment (LCA). LCA is accepted across the world as an impartial way to evaluate and compare the environmental impacts of different building materials, products and complete structures over their lifetime. It therefore combines the impacts of embodied energy already discussed, with those of building operations, maintenance and end-of-life dismantling and disposal. Whole-building LCA was introduced to North America by the Ottawa-based Athena Sustainable Materials Institute in 2002, having been in use in Europe for several years. Athena's 'Impact Estimator' can be used to compare the life cycle performance of different structural designs and building enclosure options. In 2014, Athena published its first Environmental Building Declarations (EPDs) post-occupancy evaluations of the life cycle impacts of completed buildings, analogous to the nutrition labels found on food packaging. These EBDs are compliant with the European standard EN 15978 – Sustainability of Construction Works,[4] a standard that is intended to support decision-making and documentation around the assessment of environmental performance of buildings. One of Athena's earliest EBDs was performed on the Wood Innovation and Design Centre in Prince George, Canada. (The key results from this study can be found on p. 132).
In almost every case LCA demonstrates that wood is the most environmentally responsible structural material when used in functionally appropriate applications. Thus building in wood contributes to climate change mitigation, not only through increased carbon storage, but also through the decreased GHG emissions that result if wood is used as a substitute for more energy-intensive materials.

CONCLUSION

The world's carbon cycle is a complex system and the role that forests play within it is a vital one. Despite continuing concern for the negative impacts of deforestation in the developing world, a growing body of research has confirmed that responsible human intervention, guided by the principles of sustainable forest management, can have beneficial effects.
By 2007, the scientific consensus around this position enabled the Intergovernmental Panel on Climate Change (IPCC) to conclude in its Fourth Assessment Report that 'a sustainable forest management strategy aimed at maintaining or increasing forest carbon stocks, while producing an annual sustained yield of timber fibre or energy from the forest, will generate the largest sustained mitigation benefit.'[5]

REFERENCES

1   United Nations Food and Agriculture Organization (2001). Report on the *State of the World's Forests*, 2001. Retrieved from http://www.fao.org/docrep/003/y0900e/y0900e01.htm

2   Because these species have similar properties, they are grouped together for commercial purposes under the designation SPF. The species include: white spruce (*Picea glauca*), Engelmann spruce (*Picea engelmannii*), lodgepole pine (*Pinus contorta*) and Alpine fir (*Abies lasiocarpa*).

3   As with SPF, these species are grouped together for commercial purposes because of their similar properties. The species include loblolly (*Pinus teada*), longleaf (*Pinus palustris*), shortleaf (*Pinus echinata*) and slash (*Pinus elliottii*) pines

4   Athena Sustainable Materials Institute (2014). Athena Guide to Whole Building LCA in Green Building Programs. Retrieved from http://calculatelca.com/wp-content/uploads/2014/03/Athena_Guide_to_Whole-Building_LCA_in_Green_Building_Programs_March-2014.pdf

5   Intergovernmental Panel on Climate Change (2007). *IPCC Fourth Assessment Report: Climate Change.* Retrieved from http://www.ipcc.ch/publications_and_data/ar4/wg3/en/ch9s9-es.html

BUILDING TALLER WITH WOOD

The transformation of societies throughout the world, from predominantly rural ones to predominantly urban ones, continues to gain momentum. Seen as centres of opportunity, creativity and innovation, cities are being tasked with accommodating an ever-increasing number of people. To do so economically and efficiently, without exacerbating the negative effects of urban sprawl, it is essential that cities build upward rather than outward. For this form of development to be environmentally sustainable, we must build as many of these new structures as possible using low-energy, low-carbon solutions.

However, almost everywhere in the world, current building codes require that tall buildings be built exclusively using 'non-combustible' construction, that is to say, with load-bearing structures of concrete,

masonry or steel. With its compelling environmental benefits relative to these other materials, it is imperative that wood takes its place in the construction of cities. To do so will mean changing the rules, the techniques, the perception and the economics of building Tall Wood structures.

WHY NOT WOOD?

The current impediments to the construction of Tall Wood buildings are both legislative and perceptual. In many jurisdictions, building codes have historically prescribed height and area limits for wood buildings due to concerns about their performance when exposed to fire. Such concerns are deep-rooted and, without exception, have emerged quite reasonably as a response to catastrophic fire events.

Most famously, the Great Fire of London in 1666, which destroyed 80% of the city, led to the introduction of the London Building Act, which required all buildings to be constructed of brick or stone, and was the first such regulation to include provisions for enforcement by municipal surveyors.

Two centuries later, and more central to the narrative of this book, the Great Chicago Fire of 1871 destroyed more than 17,500 buildings in the city's central business district. The extent of the damage was due to uncommonly strong winds, a summer drought and the wood construction and exterior finishes of the densely packed commercial buildings. In the aftermath, a financially shaken insurance industry lobbied the City to improve its safety standards and to mandate that all new buildings be of fireproof construction. From that point on, load-bearing masonry structures that used only brick, stone and terra-cotta were deemed compliant, and attracted the lowest insurance rates. Any deviations from this 'standard construction, including those buildings incorporating wood,' were subject to higher premiums.[1]

Against this backdrop, the introduction a decade later of reinforced concrete and steel frame construction, together with the electric elevator, offered architects and engineers a compelling, code-compliant vision of the future. Since then, high-rise construction in concrete and steel has become the universal norm.

BUILDING CODES

The building codes that emerged as a result of these and other fire events across the world were 'prescriptive'. They stipulated the use of a limited range of construction materials and assemblies deemed to satisfy the required fire and life safety standards. In so doing, they differentiated between 'combustible construction', permissible only for small, low-rise and low-hazard buildings, and 'non-combustible' construction, permissible for buildings of all sizes and types. In most cases, all-wood structures, whether light frame or heavy timber, were classified as 'combustible construction' and subject to the same restrictions.

In some jurisdictions, where it was not prohibited by code, construction in wood (if not the use of light wood exterior cladding and decorative elements) continued into the early decades of the 20th century, taking the form of heavy timber post-and-beam structures clad in masonry. More than 100 years later, among the most impressive surviving examples are: The Landing, a commercial warehouse constructed between 1905 and 1910 in the Gastown district of Vancouver, Canada, which still stands at nine storeys (two below grade and seven above); and Perry House (now the Royal Albert Hotel) in Brisbane, Australia, constructed between 1911 and 1913, originally as an eight-storey structure, to which a ninth storey was added in 1923. These buildings, and others like them, are evidence of the safety, adaptability and durability of heavy timber and (by implication) other massive wood structures in the urban context, and have become touchstones for contemporary architects and engineers.

Wood and Fire

We now know that the heavy timber members used in these historic structures, and the massive timber components of the kind used for the construction of today's Tall Wood buildings, exhibit very different behaviour when exposed to fire, than do light wood members with small sections such as those used for cladding, trim, balconies, escape ladders, etc. Full-scale testing conducted in several countries has confirmed that mass timber elements do not ignite easily, and when they do burn, it is at a slow and very predictable rate.

However, laboratory testing is just the first of many steps that must be taken to obtain industry and market acceptance of Tall Wood buildings. Most critical is the need to move away from prescriptive codes to 'objective-based' codes, which identify performance standards a building must meet, leaving the onus on the design team to demonstrate compliance. This approach, which relies on techniques such as fire simulation modelling, will be discussed in more detail in chapter 5, Building Performance, p. 41.

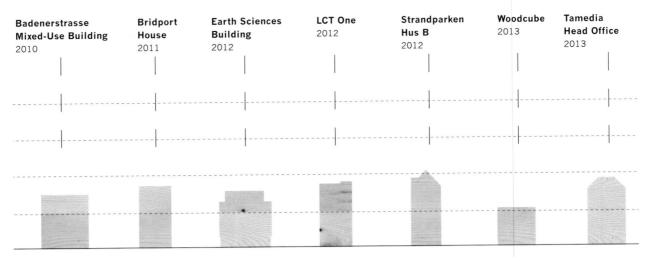

| Badenerstrasse Mixed-Use Building 2010 | Bridport House 2011 | Earth Sciences Building 2012 | LCT One 2012 | Strandparken Hus B 2012 | Woodcube 2013 | Tamedia Head Office 2013 |

A comparison of the heights of the 13 contemporary Tall Wood buildings documented in the case study section of this book next to a large Douglas fir tree

The Process of Change

Since the publication of EN1955 Eurocode 5 – Design of Timber Structures, in 2004, most European countries have moved incrementally to harmonize their regional and national building codes with this new European standard. As a result, most now have (or will soon have) objective-based building codes, and North America is moving slowly but steadily in that direction. These changes will ultimately create a framework that will support the construction of taller wood buildings, although the translation of theory into practice remains a work in progress.

While changes to building codes restricting the use of wood generally happened quickly in response to fire-related disasters, reversing these changes to reflect our emerging understanding of the material, its properties, performance and potential, is no easy matter.

As an example, Canada's first National Building Code (which was based on US precedents and published in 1941) permitted heavy timber structures up to 22.5 metres (seven storeys) in height. However, the introduction of a risk assessment approach to code development, related to fire load, building volume, and construction type, reduced this height to four storeys in 1953. The height limit was supported by local fire authorities on the basis that it represented the tallest structure in which a fire could realistically be controlled and extinguished given the firefighting equipment of the day.[2] Only now, with the widespread application and acceptance of fire simulation modelling, is the height restriction on wood buildings being lifted from four to six storeys in Canada.

Although some are further along in this process, most countries have faced similar challenges in amending

restrictive building codes, largely because these regulations are by nature conservative, and rightly rely on an exhaustive consultation process before any changes are approved. Codes are also complex instruments, regulating a suite of often inter-related building performance criteria, including structural integrity, fire safety, thermal performance and noise control. In addition, all new materials, products and assemblies referenced in building codes must be tested and certified in accordance with the appropriate national or international standards.

The aggregated effect of these parameters is to make the introduction and approval of new approaches to building a considerable challenge. In regard to the use of wood, the ways in which this challenge has been addressed have varied in detail from one regional or national jurisdiction to another. This diversity is reflected in the 13 case studies in the portfolio section, chapters 8, 9 and 10 of this book [ill. p. 22–23 above]. Most of the buildings have been preceded by extensive industry research, experimental prototypes and (in some cases) legislative tools that encourage or mandate the use of wood in publicly funded buildings.

GOVERNMENT POLICIES AND MARKET INCENTIVES

Recognizing that changing building codes can be a slow and exacting process, a number of local, regional and national governments have recently introduced policies to encourage the use of wood. Such policies generally require responsibly sourced wood to be considered as the primary construction and finishing material in all public buildings. While the overall objectives are similar, the legislative tools vary from one jurisdiction to another.

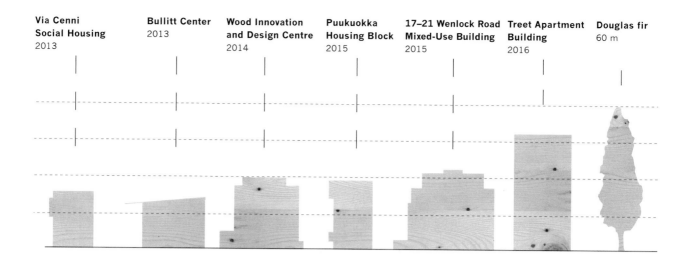

Via Cenni
Social Housing
2013

Bullitt Center
2013

Wood Innovation
and Design Centre
2014

Puukuokka
Housing Block
2015

17–21 Wenlock Road
Mixed-Use Building
2015

Treet Apartment
Building
2016

Douglas fir
60 m

In 2006, the Swedish city of Växjö, long known for its progressive environmental policies, declared its intention to accelerate the adoption of Eurocode 5 by developing a new subdivision that would become the 'Modern Wooden City'. Here, developers and design teams would be asked to consider wood as the primary building material. After successful trials with smaller-scale massive wood buildings, the city initiated the Limnologen project. Designed by Ola Malm, Arkitektbolaget, the project comprises four eight-storey apartment buildings constructed using CLT and glulam and was completed in 2009 [ill. p. 24 right]. Through a comprehensive monitoring program, Limnologen has demonstrated that industry concerns, such as structural integrity, fire protection, construction complexity and durability could be successfully addressed.

In 2009, the government of British Columbia, Canada, passed the Wood First Act, requiring that all newly constructed publicly funded buildings such as schools, libraries or sports complexes, consider wood as the primary building material. In France, the national legislation is prescriptive and requires all new public buildings to include 0.2 cubic metres of wood for every square metre of building floor area.

In the Netherlands, legislation makes it compulsory to provide environmental impact information for all new buildings, a requirement that tends to favour wood products. In the United Kingdom, the so-called 'Merton Rule' (which began as a municipal bylaw in 2008, and is now embedded in national regulations) requires all new commercial buildings over 1000 square metres to meet 10% of their operating energy needs from renewable sources. While this may seem a straightforward requirement that encourages solar panels and wind turbines, this rule, like objective-based codes, is open to interpretation. During the design of the nine-storey Murray Grove apartment building in London, England, architects Waugh Thistleton argued that, if the building were to be constructed of massive wood panels, the carbon stored in the structure would have a greater environmental benefit than providing 10% renewable energy to operate a building made of concrete. An 'equivalency' to the Merton Rule was granted, and in 2009 Murray Grove became the world's first modern Tall Wood building [ill. p. 24 left].

Harnessing Market Forces

In addition to legislative tools and incentives, some of the impetus for change has come from the recognition of the unique sustainable attributes of wood, and the contribution it can make toward compliance with increasingly influential voluntary green building standards.

The first such program was Passive House, developed in Germany in the late 1980s. It was designed to promote the creation of low-energy buildings that would require approximately 90% less input energy for space heating and cooling than a conventionally designed equivalent. As a voluntary standard, Passive House was the first significant attempt to reduce the ecological footprint of buildings through non-regulatory market incentives. Like many others that have followed, the Passive House standard implicitly (though not explicitly) promotes the use of wood.

For Passive House, the first objective is the creation of a highly insulated building envelope that minimizes heat loss through thermal bridging. The low thermal conductivity of structural wood elements, makes wood an advantageous choice of material for Passive House structures, including Tall Wood buildings such as LCT

Waugh Thistleton, the architects of the Murray Grove apartments in London, England were able to demonstrate that a solid wood building would have a lower life cycle carbon footprint than a concrete building in which 10% of the operating energy was generated from renewable sources.

The Limnologen housing project, by Arkitektbolaget, 2009, in Växjö, Sweden, is part of the 'Modern Wooden City', a new suburb that encouraged the early adoption of Eurocode 5 – Design of Timber Buildings.

One in Dornbirn, Austria [pp. 142–151] and Treet in Bergen, Norway [pp. 158–163].

For its part, the US-based 'Living Building Challenge' (LBC) promotes wood implicitly because of its ability to sequester and store carbon. LBC was launched in 2006 by the non-profit International Living Future Institute (ILFI). According to ILFI, Living Buildings are designed to operate 'as cleanly, beautifully and efficiently as nature's architecture.'[3] Among the prerequisites that a building must meet to achieve certification, is carbon-neutral construction.

Although this may theoretically be achieved through various forms of carbon offset, most projects certified so far, including the Bullitt Center in Seattle, USA [pp. 118–123], have chosen to use substantial quantities of wood.

CONCLUSION

In the face of increasing urbanization, and the densification of our cities, Tall Wood buildings represent the most practical, effective and environmentally responsible solution to the global housing shortage. To enable the widespread implementation of Tall Wood buildings, it is necessary to adopt objective-based building codes, introduce legislation supporting or mandating low-carbon construction, and to capitalize on market-based incentive programs.

While the newly developed range of engineered wood products and computerized manufacturing techniques that will be described in subsequent chapters, have transformed the capabilities and potential of the wood industry, empirical evidence in the form of completed Tall Wood structures is what will ultimately transform the marketplace.

REFERENCES

1   Sereca Consulting Inc. (2015). *The Historical Development of Building Size Limits in the National Building Code of Canada.* Retrieved from http://cwc.ca/wp-content/uploads/2015/04/HistoricalDevelopment-BldgSizeLimits-NBCC-2015-s.pdf

2   Seneca Consulting Inc. (2015). *Historical Development of Building Size Limits in the National Building Code of Canada.* Retrieved from http://cwc.ca/wp-content/uploads/2015/04/HistoricalDevelopment-BldgSizeLimits-NBCC-2015-s.pdf

3   International Living Future Institute (2006). *The Living Building Challenge.* Retrieved from http://living-future.org/lbc

MATERIALS

The barriers to building taller with wood have been both legislative and perceptual. Even as prescriptive building codes give way to objective-based ones, concerns about the strength and durability of wood remain – if not with architects and engineers, then with approving authorities, developers and the public. After all, the wood with which they are familiar is a soft, organic material, susceptible both to physical damage by fire and to decay if allowed to remain wet for a prolonged period of time.

While this may be true for solid sawn material in its natural state, the properties and performance of wood can be modified to a significant degree by modern processing methods. Engineered massive wood products, such as cross-laminated timber (CLT), laminated veneer lumber (LVL), laminated strand lumber (LSL) and parallel strand lumber (PSL), are now available alongside glue-laminated timber (glulam), and are stronger, more consistent and more dimensionally stable than traditional solid sawn material. However, even with these modified properties, an understanding of the intrinsic characteristics of wood remains critical to the successful design of Tall Wood buildings.

PROPERTIES OF WOOD

Most important among the properties of wood is the fact that, as an organic material with a cellular structure, its strength and stability vary with orientation of grain and moisture content. Controlling these two variables is key to creating components and structures that are precise, dimensionally stable, strong and ultimately more durable.

Bound and Free Moisture

Wood contains two types of moisture in liquid form: free moisture and bound moisture. The structure of wood fibre is often compared to a cluster of drinking straws, and this analogy can assist us to understand the difference. Bound moisture is the moisture that is naturally contained within the cell walls (or within the casing of the straw itself) and is chemically bonded to the wood. Free (or capillary) moisture is the moisture that is contained between the cell walls (or within the tubular centre of the straw) and is held in the wood only by capillary forces. It constitutes the greater part of the moisture present in 'green' wood from newly felled trees.

The moisture content (MC) for a given sample of wood is defined as the weight of water in the wood expressed as a percentage of the 'dry' weight of the wood itself. This 'dry' weight is considered to be the weight of the sample after oven drying under standardized conditions of temperature and time. For reference purposes, a living tree or freshly cut log may have a moisture content in excess of 50%, air drying may bring this down to less than 20% and kiln drying to as little as 8%.

Wood is hygroscopic, and will absorb or release moisture to maintain a state of balance with the surrounding environment. If 'green' lumber is installed into the controlled temperature and humidity conditions of a building, the wood will release moisture until it re-establishes a state of equilibrium with this new environment. Typically, this will happen at a moisture content of between 8 and 12% depending on the climate of the region and the season of the year. At this point, the wood is said to have reached its equilibrium moisture content (EMC).

Moisture Movement

As moisture is released, the wood shrinks. That shrinkage is approximately 1% for every 5% reduction in moisture content perpendicular to grain, and approximately one tenth of this value parallel to grain. For a single wood member, this may not seem to be much

of a problem – 2–3mm when a 100mm thick member dries from an MC of 25% to its installed EMC – but cumulatively, the effect can be significant. Even in small buildings, it is preferable to specify lumber that has been 'surfaced dry' (that is, allowed to air-dry to a lower moisture content before being planed to its final size), as this reduces the amount of shrinkage that will be experienced in service.

In Tall Wood buildings, even more attention must be paid to the specification of materials and products, and to designing a structural system that will minimize the effects of moisture movement and shrinkage. Therefore almost all material used in Tall Wood buildings is kiln-dried.

Kiln Drying

Kiln drying is done using specially designed ovens in which the wood is stacked on racks that permit air circulation around each member. The temperature is carefully controlled to ensure that drying does not occur too quickly and potentially causes warping or uneven shrinkage. Kiln drying can be used to reduce the moisture content of wood to any desired value, with a target of 12% being typical. In addition to reducing the volume of material through shrinkage, drying also increases the strength of wood members.

Strength

Different species of wood have different characteristics of strength, dimensional stability and weather resistance, making the choice of species an important one. In North America, Alaskan yellow cedar (*Cupressus nootkatensis*) and western red cedar (*Thuja plicata*) are typically used for exterior applications, and Douglas fir (*Pseudotsuga menziesii*) and southern yellow pine species are chosen when superior strength is required. In Central Europe, Norway spruce (*Picea abies*) and Scots pine (*Pinus sylvestris*) are the most common species for structural applications, while European larch (*Larix decidua*) is generally used for exterior cladding. The strength of a building material is a measure of that material's ability to withstand a given load with-

Glue-laminated timber (glulam) is fabricated by gluing individual pieces of dimensional lumber together to form columns, beams and headers.

out failure. The different types of load to which a structural component may be subjected are: compression, tension, bending, shear and torsion. The strength of wood varies according to the direction in which a force is applied to it. The material is strongest in tension and compression parallel to grain (that is when the force is applied along the fibres), and much weaker (typically by a factor of ten) when the force is applied perpendicular or tangential to grain.

The strength of wood varies between species: western red cedar may have a compressive strength of around 1100kPa (kilo Pascals), Douglas fir a strength of around 1800kPa and mahogany a strength of around 3600kPa. In addition, the natural variability of wood (which may include tighter or more open grain, as well as the presence of minor defects such as splits, checks and knots) means that for solid sawn wood products there can be considerable variation in these figures. Since this inconsistency of natural wood makes the predictability of performance difficult, wood industry researchers around the world have spent decades on the development of engineered wood products (EWPs), with the aim of increasing the strength of wood and reducing variation.

ENGINEERED WOOD PRODUCTS

EWPs are manufactured by bonding together wood strands, veneers, small sections of solid lumber or other forms of wood fibre to produce a larger and integral composite unit that is stronger and stiffer than the sum of its parts.

The material that makes up engineered wood products can generally be obtained from smaller trees, and the manufacturing process enables a much greater per-

centage of the tree to be used than would be possible with solid sawn lumber. In addition, because the wood or wood fibre used in the manufacturing process is kiln-dried, engineered wood products, are dimensionally stable and can be fabricated to precise specifications. The two most familiar EWPs are plywood and glulam, both of which have been in common use since the early 1900s. In the last three decades, they have been joined by a range of new massive wood products, which (like glulams) lend themselves to the construction of Tall Wood buildings.

Accordingly, the descriptions that follow relate to the massive panel and beam products used in Tall Wood construction. Because these products are manufactured under controlled conditions using a variety of bonding and pressing techniques, they can typically be produced in a range of standard thicknesses, in widths up to 2.5 or 3.0 metres, and in lengths limited only by the constraints of road transportation.

Glue-Laminated Timber

Glulam [ill. p. 27 above] is manufactured by gluing together individual pieces of dimension lumber under controlled conditions to form larger linear elements. In Tall Wood buildings glulam is used for columns, beams, headers, and in the case of Treet [pp. 158–163] both vertical and horizontal trusses were fabricated from glulam.

While the process of glulam fabrication remains fundamentally the same as when first introduced in Germany in 1906, the lumber used today is a select high-strength grade, known as 'lamstock'. Lamstock is available in three grades, the highest being L1 and the lowest being L3.

Laminated veneer lumber (LVL) is fabricated by laminating and gluing multiple veneers together in the same orientation. This enables long elements to be produced that have high strength in one direction.

Laminated strand lumber (LSL) is fabricated from flaked wood strands glued together in large billets. The length is limited only by standard shipping and trucking dimensions. LSL can be used for floors, walls and vertical members where large floor-to-floor heights are required.

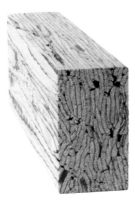

Parallel strand lumber (PSL) is fabricated from long strands of veneer pressed and glued into standard dimensions and lengths. It has very consistent properties and high strength.

In North America, glulam has traditionally been made from Douglas fir, SPF (spruce/pine/fir), larch (*Larix decidua*) or southern yellow pine. However for exterior applications it is now possible to obtain glulam made from Alaskan yellow cedar. In Northern Europe and Russia, red pine (*Pinus resinosa*) and white spruce are the most common species used for the manufacture of glulam.

Lamstock is typically supplied in nominal thicknesses of 25 or 34mm and (according to species and country of origin) widths of 80 to 170mm. Lengths are typically 3 metres or longer, with pieces being finger-jointed and glued together as necessary. The lamstock is kiln-dried to a moisture content of between 10 and 14%, then end-glued together to attain the required length. The multiple laminations are then face-glued together under pressure in a jig that (if required) gives the final product the desired camber, curvature or taper. Glulams can be fabricated to any length, enabling them to be used for long free spans, or continuous spans over multiple points of support. They can also be used for columns that extend over multiple floors. Glulam beams are normally laid up so that they are in the vertical orientation when loaded (i.e. the load is applied perpendicular to the long face of the laminations). In such cases, the upper and lower laminations may be specified to have a higher strength class than the centre laminations, as these are the parts of the beam where compressive and tensile forces are greatest.

Nordic, an engineered wood products manufacturer in northern Quebec makes glue-laminated products using small-dimension square sections cut from the tips of black spruce trees. The sections are then glued together both horizontally and vertically to make glulam beams, columns and panels that have a distinctive checkerboard cross section. This material was used for the columns, beams and floor panels of the six-storey Fondaction CSN Building in Quebec City, designed by GHA – Gilles Huot Architecte and completed in 2010 [ill. p. 34]. Glulam can be supplied in a variety of appearance grades for concealed or exposed applications, and can be pressure treated for exterior use when bonded with waterproof glues.

Glue-Laminated Timber Panels
Glue-laminated timber panels [ill. p. 31 bottom left] have the appearance of glulam beams laid horizontally and are generally available from glulam manufacturers in the same range of species used for regular glulam beams.

GLT panels have one-directional spanning capability and are combined with plywood sheathing if lateral resistance is required. Care must be taken with respect to swelling and shrinkage perpendicular to grain. GLT panels can be used for floors, walls and roofs. Unlike glulam beams, GLT panels are designed to resist loads applied parallel to the long face of the laminations, and thus all the lamstock in a given panel will be of the same structural grade.

Laminated Veneer Lumber

Laminated veneer lumber [ill. p. 28 top] is produced by bonding thin wood veneers together in a large billet so that the grain of all veneers is parallel to the long direction. Because LVL is made with scarfed or lapped jointed veneers, LVL is available in lengths far beyond conventional lumber lengths. As a structural panel product, it is uniform in appearance and highly predictable in performance.

The veneers used in LVL are dried and graded (similar to plywood) and bonded with waterproof glues. Unlike plywood however, the veneers run vertically through the thickness of the panel rather than being laid horizontally. Because knots, slope of grain and splits have been dispersed throughout the material or eliminated altogether, LVL is virtually free from warping and splitting.

In its standard form (in which all veneers have the same orientation), LVL can be cut for use as beams and headers, or left in panel form for floors, walls and roofs. When diaphragm action is required to resist lateral forces, joints between panels can be detailed to transfer these loads.

LVL can also be manufactured with approximately 20% of the veneers oriented so their grain is perpendicular to that of the other veneers in the billet. This partially cross-laminated panel has greater crushing strength than conventional LVL panels. LVL can be made from a number of different wood species, including Douglas fir (*Douglas abies*) and lodgepole pine (*Pinus contorta*).

Laminated Strand Lumber

Laminated strand lumber [ill. p. 28 centre] is made from flaked wood strands that have a length-to-thickness ratio of approximately 150. The strands used in LSL typically come from fast-growing aspen (*Populus remuloides*) or tulip poplar (*Liriodendron tuipitera*), and are arranged parallel to the longitudinal axis of the panel. This gives LSL panels one-directional spanning capability.

Combined with an adhesive, the oriented strands are formed into a large mat or billet and pressed. In Tall Wood buildings, LSL can be used as floor, wall and roof paneling, as well as for vertical members in situations where the floor-to-floor heights are substantial, and the wind loads are significant. The panels come in a range of standard thicknesses and a maximum width of 2.4 metres. Like other engineered wood products LSL offers predictable strength, good moisture resistance and dimensional stability that minimizes twisting and shrinkage.

Parallel Strand Lumber

Parallel strand lumber [ill. p. 28 bottom] was developed in Canada in the 1980s by MacMillan Bloedel (now Weyerhaeuser Company Ltd). As such, it is a proprietary product marketed under the trade name Parallam®. PSL is manufactured from veneers clipped into long strands laid in parallel formation and bonded together under pressure with an adhesive to form the finished structural section. The length-to-thickness ratio of the strands in PSL is around 300. It is produced in billets that have a maximum cross section of 400mm × 400mm.

PSL is manufactured in Canada from Douglas fir and in the United States from southern pine. Because the growth imperfections have been removed from the wood strands prior to fabrication, PSL products have consistent properties and high load-carrying capacity. In Tall Wood buildings, PSL can be used for posts and beams, particularly where high bending strength is required, as well as for incidental beams, headers and lintels in load-bearing panel construction.

PSL readily accepts preservative treatment and therefore protection from moisture damage is possible. Treated PSL should be specified for members that will be directly exposed to high humidity conditions. Visually, PSL is attractive, so it is suited to applications where finished appearance is important.

Cross-Laminated Timber

Cross-laminated timber [ill. p. 31 top left] is comprised of multiple layers of boards stacked together, with alternating layers at right angles to one another. Layers are bonded to form a composite panel, most often using glue. The glue may be applied either on the faces of each board or on both the faces and edges. Boards may also be finger-jointed and glued in the longitudinal direction.

CLT panels can also be fabricated using mechanical fasteners rather than adhesives. Nails driven at opposing angles through multiple layers can achieve the required structural performance, as can wooden dowels inserted into pre-drilled holes. In the latter case, the dowels are of a different species (often beech) and dried to a lower moisture content than the panel. When the dowels expand to achieve their equilibrium moisture content, they create an ultra-tight fit capable of holding the panel layers together under load. Whatever the fastening method, the result is a product that has good dimensional stability and (in case of five layers or more in thickness) two-way spanning capability.

CLT panels are fabricated with an odd number of layers (typically three to seven) so that the outermost layers have the same orientation of grain. For situations in which special load-carrying capabilities are required, adjacent layers may be placed in the same direction – typically resulting in a double layer at the faces or core of the panel.

The lumber used is kiln-dried; thicknesses of individual pieces may vary from 16mm to 51mm, and the width from 60mm to 240mm. Panel sizes vary by manufacturer; typical widths being 0.6 metres, 1.2 metres, 2.4 metres and 3.0 metres. The outer layers of CLT wall panels are usually oriented with the grain running vertically in the direction of the applied loads. Similarly, the grain in the upper and lower layers of floor and roof panels is usually oriented parallel to the longer span. As with glulam, CLT may be supplied in either an architectural grade (with outer layers selected for their appearance) or a structural grade (designed to be concealed behind a surface finish).

Nail-Laminated Timber

Nail-laminated timber panels [ill. p. 31 right] are made up of regular solid sawn framing members (2 × 4, 2 × 6 inches, etc.) arranged side by side on edge, and fastened together with nails or lag screws. They can be made from a variety of species including Douglas fir and SPF. Specification is based on the grade of solid sawn material used, and there are no applicable standards for the fabricated panels themselves.

Unlike other massive timber products, NLT does not need capital investment in specialized manufacturing facilities and can be fabricated by experienced carpenters in a conventional wood shop. NLT panels require plywood or other sheathing for lateral resistance and, because they have no continuous glue layers, they use additional sealing on site to prevent the passage of smoke or other fumes through the floor assembly. NLT

Cross-laminated timber (CLT) is created by laminating dimensional lumber in layers that are perpendicular to one another. The resulting panels have two-way spanning capability, are dimensionally stable and are suitable for walls, roofs and floors.

Nail-laminated timber panels are similar to glulam equivalents but the individual pieces are nailed together rather than glued. This creates an economical panel product that can be fabricated without expensive equipment and that offers one-way spanning capability.

Glue-laminated timber panels have the appearance of glulam beams laid flat. These panels provide a strong and economical flooring option with one-way spanning capability.

is more vulnerable to mould and other water-related damage than engineered wood equivalents, and considerable care must be taken to protect the end grain in particular from prolonged exposure to moisture.

ADHESIVES

With the exception of mechanically fastened CLT and NLT panels, the engineered massive wood products listed above are bonded using formaldehyde-based glues. The type of glue depends on the temperature of the process, on whether the product is for interior or exterior use and on whether the finished appearance of the product is important (some glues are clear, others dark in colour).

Most structural adhesives contain formaldehyde. Formaldehyde is a naturally occurring organic compound that is present in wood and wood products. Environmental standards related to indoor air quality are aimed at limiting the outgassing of formaldehyde and other volatile organic compounds (VOCs) as at higher concentrations they can be harmful to health. Different adhesive formulations contain different concentrations of formaldehyde and research is ongoing to develop low- and no-formaldehyde glues. The percentage of glue by weight in the glue-bonded massive

wood products described above varies from 1% in glulam beams and GLT panels, to 6 or 7% in LSL and PSL. As a general rule, the dimensional stability and moisture resistance of products increases with the percentage of glue by weight.

CONCLUSION

Architects and structural engineers have a wide range of mass panel and beam products at their disposal that can meet the specific performance requirements of Tall Wood buildings. It is crucial to understand the different properties of each material or product to optimize its use for a specific application. Furthermore, while engineered products reduce the variability associated with solid sawn lumber, they do not eliminate it entirely. It remains of critical importance to understand the characteristics of moisture movement and shrinkage, which must still be addressed to ensure that a Tall Wood building performs as designed.

STRUCTURAL SYSTEMS

Structural design is concerned with the strength, rigidity and stability of structures. Whatever the materials employed, the fundamental objective is to create a structure capable of resisting all the loads, and meeting the other functional requirements to which it will be subjected during its service life, without suffering premature deterioration or failure.

Loads may be vertical (as with the self-weight of the building, the imposed load of snow on the roof, or the weight of furniture, fittings and building occupants); or lateral (as with wind loads, which may result in positive or negative pressure on opposing faces of the building). In earthquake-prone areas, seismic forces must also be taken into consideration. Seismic waves travel either in the body of the Earth or at the surface, and the forces they apply to buildings may be either

lateral or vertical. Other external forces to which buildings may be subjected include hydrostatic pressure from soils and/or groundwater, and uplift from wind.

LOAD PATHS

These external forces, and the others applied by the live (occupant and equipment) loads within the building, may result in individual structural members or building elements being subjected to compression, tension, bending, torsion or shear. The structure must be designed so that all these forces can be resolved and transmitted, through the horizontal and vertical elements of structure, to the ground.

One of the most important considerations in the design of Tall Wood buildings is to account for shrinkage. This is particularly important when detailing the vertical elements of the structure, as excessive or un-equal shrinkage can affect the elevation and alignment of key building elements, and even compromise the integrity of the building envelope. The best approach is to design a vertical structure in which all wood grain is parallel to the load path, either by superimposing vertical elements directly on top of one another, or by devising connection details that bypass or minimize the effects of any cross grain in the vertical section.

Vertical Loads

Ideally, vertical loads should be carried through con-tinuous or superimposed structural elements, whether posts or panels. Substantial offsets in the vertical load path will require special structural details, such as transfer trusses, as in the Earth Sciences Building [pp. 102–107] or transfer beams, as at Bridport House [pp. 64–69].

Tall Wood structures may be constructed as platform systems or as balloon systems. In platform systems, the vertical load-carrying elements (whether posts or panels) are one storey in height, and each floor forms a platform for the construction of the next. When CLT is used in platform construction, it is desirable to de-vise a detail that will reduce crushing or shrinkage of the floor panels that are subject to loads perpendicu-lar to grain.

The aim is to transfer a portion of the vertical load directly from the upper to the lower wall panel. This can be done by drilling holes through the floor panel and filling them with wood dowels, steel pipes or concrete, as at Via Cenni in Milan, Italy [pp. 76–81]. An alternative approach is to castellate the wall panels to create an end grain-to-end grain bearing condition, which at the same time can provide support for the floor panels, as at Bridport House.

When a platform system is constructed using a post-and-beam frame, a similar detail is necessary to create an end grain-to-end grain bearing condition between the posts of one storey and the posts of the next. This condition may be achieved using a steel spacer that is

the same depth as the floor slab, as in the Bullitt Cen-ter [pp. 118–123]; or by notching the columns to cre-ate shoulders upon which the beams can rest, as in the Fondaction CSN Building in Quebec City [ill. p. 34]. An alternative approach is to connect the beam direct-ly into the column using a proprietary concealed con-nector, as at the Wood Innovation and Design Centre [pp. 124–133]; or by twinning the beams so that they run past the columns on either side.

Lateral Loads

Lateral loads can be resisted in the vertical plane by rigid (moment) frames, braced frames or shear walls located at the building perimeter. Shear walls can be at intervals throughout the building or grouped within strong vertical cores such as elevator or stair shafts – or in a combination of all three locations as the design permits. Lateral systems must generally be used in both directions (east–west and north–south in a build-ing aligned to the cardinal points of the compass) and ideally be evenly spaced throughout the floor plan.

To act in unison, these brace frame and shear wall ele-ments must be connected together by rigid horizontal 'diaphragms' – either floors, roofs or both. The entire lateral system must be anchored in such a way as to transfer the applied lateral loads to the ground. This function is often performed by stair or elevator shafts or by continuous vertical brace frames extending the full height of the building.

LOAD TRANSFER

In multi-storey projects the lateral system should ide-ally be consistent from one floor to the next, so that the cross bracing or shear walls are in the same verti-cal plane. Cross bracing was used in the Bullitt Center [ill. p. 35], and the use of vertically aligned CLT shear walls was most rigorously applied in the Via Cenni project.

Both of these projects include concrete stair and elevator shafts that serve to transfer lateral loads down to concrete podium structures. This system is also used at LCT One, where the composite concrete

The vertical posts in the Fondaction CSN Building in Quebec City, 2010, designed by GHA – Gilles Huot Architecte, are notched to create bearing surfaces for its twinned beams.

and glulam floor panels are bolted together to form a diaphragm, which is connected by steel brackets to a concrete stair and elevator core.

From a structural point of view, stair and elevator cores need not necessarily be constructed of concrete. Indeed, a CLT core was used at the Wood Innovation and Design Centre [pp. 124–133], where the panels were fabricated with a half-lap profile that enabled them to be lag screwed together. This created continuous vertical shear walls, with the lag screw and hold down connections providing the necessary ductility (see section on ductility below).

The choice of a wood or concrete core will depend on a number of factors, including economy, efficiency, preference of the structural engineer and in some cases the requirements of local fire codes. Where concrete cores are used, consideration must be given to the potential for differential movement between the wood and concrete elements of the structure. This may require the use of slip joints to accommodate vertical movement and adjustable thresholds at stair and elevator doors.

DUCTILITY

Ductility (the ability of a material to deform under stress, thus absorbing and dissipating energy) is an important aspect of structural design. In Tall Wood buildings, in which the structural elements are inherently rigid, it is the connections that must perform this function. Under normal conditions, these connections are designed to behave elastically, absorbing moderate wind or seismic forces without permanent deformation. In the case of major windstorms or earthquake events however, these same connections are designed to perform 'plasticly', absorbing the applied forces through deformation, permitting minor damage to the structure but preventing the catastrophic collapse of the building.

SELF-CENTERING STRUCTURES

A new and innovative approach to the seismic design of Tall Wood buildings is that of self-centering structures. Developed by a team of engineers at the University of Canterbury, New Zealand, Pres-Lam is a proprietary post-and-beam system in which post-tensioned rods passing through hollow LVL beams are anchored to steel plates that are attached to LVL posts, creating a 'rocker' connection. These connections [ill. p. 36] are designed to deflect elastically under moderate seismic loads, but to return to their original configuration when the loads are removed. This system, which has been used successfully in the Nelson Marlborough Institute of Technology in Nelson, New Zealand (designed by Irving Smith Jack Architects and completed in 2010), and in the Te Ara Hihiko/College of Creative Arts in Wellington, New Zealand (designed by Athfield Architects and completed in 2012), greatly reduces the likelihood of structural failure. Because the tension rods are readily accessible, the Pres-Lam system also makes the evaluation and repair of damaged structures much easier. In 2015, an exclusive license was granted to Canada's FP Innovations for the use of the Pres-Lam system in North America. Its first application will be in MGA | Michael Green Architecture's OSU Forest Science Complex in Corvallis, Oregon, scheduled for completion in 2018.

The Bullitt Center in Seattle, Washington, uses a system of steel chevron braces to provide the required lateral resistance for its post-and-beam frame structure.

UPLIFT FORCES

Being light, and thus having a relatively low mass of inertia, wood structures can accelerate quickly under wind gusts that can be uncomfortable to occupants. This behaviour, and the uplift forces it can generate, must also be considered in the design of Tall Wood structures. Strategies to cope with uplift forces vary according to structural system, budget and local construction practice.

The exterior trusses at Treet [pp. 158–163] are supplemented by lateral storey-height trusses and precast concrete floors at the fifth and tenth storeys. These floors form a diaphragm that distributes the lateral loads evenly between the various vertical structural elements, and also provides a horizontal fire separation between the light frame prefabricated units.

The concrete floors, also improve the dynamic performance of the building under strong wind conditions. The vertical truss structure, combined with the added weight of the concrete floors, is sufficient to resist these wind forces – the truss on the windward side of the building being subject to tension, and the truss on the leeward side being subject to compression. The whole system is anchored by steel brackets to a concrete podium structure that accommodates the parking garage.

Using a system pioneered in the Limnologen project in 2009, uplift forces at Strandparken Hus B [pp. 70–75] are resisted by continuous steel anchor rods that run within the walls from the concrete roof of the parking garage to the top of the building.

For the Wood Innovation and Design Centre [pp. 124–133] an alternative approach was taken in which the vertical CLT panels of the service cores resist the uplift forces. These panels are connected to the concrete foundations using a combination of shear brackets and hold-down anchors. The shear brackets are connected using self-tapping screws, while the hold-down anchors are epoxy-glued using the ductile HSK system.

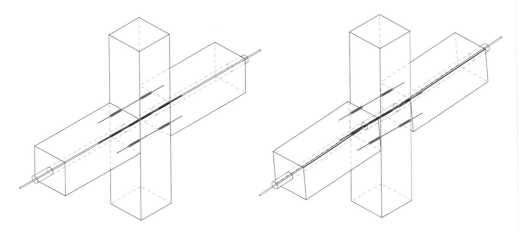

The Pres-Lam system was developed in New Zealand to improve the seismic performance of heavy timber post-and-beam structures. Steel tendons pass through hollow LVL beams and are post-tensioned to anchor plates on the LVL posts. This enables the structure to rock when subjected to moderate seismic forces, then centre itself again when the forces are removed.

STRUCTURE AND PROGRAM

Beyond the fundamental parameters of strength and stability, there are multiple other factors that will influence, if not determine, the choice of structural system. Most important is the function of the building, as this will potentially impact the spatial arrangement and need for flexibility, the length of clear spans, the structural fire resistance, and occupant-related live load requirements.

For Tall Wood buildings, a basic differentiation of function can be made between residential and commercial (or institutional) occupancies. Generally speaking, residential buildings will be more compartmented, with the consequent opportunity for a system of bearing walls to be introduced. By contrast, commercial buildings generally require flexible, open floor plans that are more easily achieved using a system of bearing posts connected by beams.

Massive Timber Panel Systems

The most familiar example of the highly compartmented approach to load-bearing construction in CLT is that of Murray Grove in England, introduced in chapter 2, Building Taller with Wood, pp. 23–24. In this project, which includes three storeys of social housing and five storeys of market housing, all interior walls are load-bearing CLT. This compartmentation in part reflects the belief that little or no reconfiguration will be necessary over the life of the building, but also creates a structure with a high degree of redundancy that meets the local regulations for the prevention of progressive collapse. Another notable example is the apartment complex Wagramerstrasse in Vienna,

designed by Schluder Architektur and completed in 2014. At seven storeys, it is Austria's tallest CLT residential building to date [ills. p. 37].

Of the projects featured in this book load-bearing wall systems were used for Bridport House [pp. 64–69], Via Cenni [pp. 76–81] and Strandparken Hus B [pp. 70–75]. The Puukuokka Housing Block [pp. 94–99] also uses a system of load-bearing CLT walls, but these are factory-built into volumetric units that are then stacked on site. All these projects have a primary residential use.

Post-and-Beam Systems

By contrast, post-and-beam systems are used in all the projects where the primary use is commercial or institutional. These include the Wood Innovation and Design Centre [pp. 124–133], the Earth Sciences Building [pp. 102–107], the Bullitt Center [pp. 118–123], the Tamedia Head Office in Zurich, Switzerland [pp. 108–117], and LCT One [pp. 142–151].

Hybrid Systems

Structural design is also concerned with efficiency and economy of means, thus all-wood structures may not always be the optimal or functionally most appropriate solution. Hybrid systems, in which steel or concrete are used for certain elements, and wood for others, are common. The strength of steel may be advantageous for heavy load conditions, whereas concrete may be used for its thermal mass, compressive strength or impact resistance. In many buildings, it is used for the basement and ground floor structure, creating a podium upon which a lighter weight (and sometimes shorter span) building is constructed.

The Wagramerstrasse apartment complex in Vienna, Austria, 2014, by Schluder Architektur, is a notable example of mass timber panel construction. The building uses CLT panels for its walls, floors and roof creating a honeycomb structure capable of resisting both vertical and lateral loads.

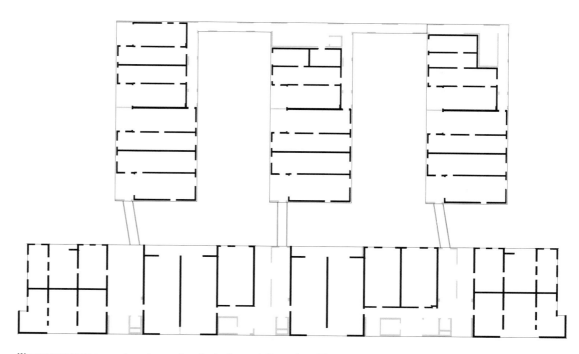

Wagramerstrasse apartment complex, typical upper floor plan. The compartmentalized structure visible in the plan is a result of the regular layout of the structural CLT walls.

The E3 mixed-use building in Berlin, Germany, 2008, by Kaden Klingbeil Architekten, has a hybrid concrete, steel and wood structure, in which the wall panels are site-built from multiple laminations of solid timber members.

17–21 Wenlock Road Mixed-Use Building in London, England, 2015, by Hawkins\Brown, has a primary structure of steel columns and beams supporting a secondary structure of CLT floor, wall and roof panels.

Sometimes hybrid structures arise in response to a regulatory requirement, particular architectural ambitions, or local practice conventions. For example, a local code (or the fire authority charged with interpreting it) may require non-combustible construction to be used for stair and elevator shafts, as was the case in LCT One [pp. 142–151].

Elsewhere, the demands of the architecture may prevail, leading to a hybrid solution. A part frame, part load-bearing structure was used at 17–21 Wenlock Road in London, England [ill. p. 38 right; see also pp. 152–157], where the steel frame supports offsets and cantilevers on successive floors, and for the Woodcube [pp. 82–93], where steel was used to stiffen the beams extending from the central core to support the exterior balconies.

Another example of hybrid construction is E3, a sevenstorey mixed-use commercial and residential building in Berlin, Germany, designed by Kaden Klingbeil Architekten and completed in 2008 [ill. p. 38 left]. E3 includes office space on the ground floor and residential units above.

The structure comprises a glulam post-and-beam frame connected with heavy steel fasteners, and two large concrete beams that span the length of the building. Structural infill walls are solid edge-laminated dowelled wood panels, and floor panels are a hybrid wood-concrete system. Exit stairs are contained within concrete shafts that stand free of the building and are connected to it by bridges.

By contrast, the Wood Innovation and Design Centre [pp. 124–133] took a philosophical approach, the intent being to showcase the versatility of wood, as well as to create a building with the lowest possible environmental impact. However, there was also the very practical consideration of avoiding non-wood materials in order to minimize the time-consuming interfaces between different structural trades on site, and so meet the very tight construction schedule.

CONCLUSION

As architects, engineers, building and fire authorities become more familiar with Tall Wood construction, the approaches described above will be supplemented by others yet to be imagined. Because of the variety and versatility of hybrid wood and steel, or wood and concrete systems, it is most likely that these will constitute the majority of structures to be built in the future.

However, as the Wood Innovation and Design Centre reminds us, it is important not to lose sight of the considerable environmental advantages of wood, and to promote its use wherever functionally appropriate and permitted by code.

BUILDING PERFORMANCE

In theory, the transition from prescriptive building codes to objective-based ones will enable designers to choose materials and propose solutions that meet the performance criteria of the relevant code, and to demonstrate compliance by calculation and simulation. In practice, most approving authorities still have perceptual barriers they must overcome before Tall Wood buildings can fulfil their potential. This chapter addresses these concerns in relation to fire safety, acoustic performance and building enclosure design.

FIRE SAFETY

Misconceptions about fire performance remain the most significant impediment to the more widespread adoption of Tall Wood technology. These misconceptions are often based on experience with fires in light-wood frame structures, as opposed to those of heavy timber or engineered massive timber construction (often shortened to 'mass timber'). Prescriptive building codes consider both these systems as 'combustible construction' – although in reality they behave very differently when exposed to fire.

Prescriptive and Performance-Based Codes

A prescriptive building code stipulates how a building must be built, rather than how it should perform, the implicit assumption being that there is only one way to meet the required standard. For decades clients, architects, engineers, insurance companies and authorities having jurisdiction found it expedient for reasons of economy, familiarity or liability, to simply build in accordance with the methods prescribed in the code.

However, such codes do generally have their basis in performance requirements, though these might not be immediately apparent. For example, the reason for prescribing a particular level of structural fire resistance is to ensure that the structure will remain stable and carry the loads for which it was designed, long enough to enable building occupants to escape, and firefighters to access the building without fear of it collapsing. Beyond the paramount concern for stability of the structure, other important performance goals, expressed as functional statements, include restricting the spread of fire, reducing exposure to occupants and limiting damage to property. Whether the philosophical approach of the code is prescriptive or performance-based, the functional demands (especially those relating to structural fire resistance) increase according to the size, occupancy and height of the building. In most jurisdictions the threshold for tall buildings is six to eight storeys, at which point the structural fire resistance requirement generally doubles from one hour to two hours. A prescriptive code will always specify such a building to be of non-combustible construction.

Alternative Solutions
Under these circumstances, the only recourse for a designer wishing to use wood is to propose an 'alternative solution'. The first step in this process is to 'unpack' the prescriptive code requirements in order to uncover the underlying intentions and objectives, and understand the risks to life safety and building integrity that they are designed to address. In countries where prescriptive codes are still in force, this 'unpacking' process creates an objective framework and establishes a baseline for the assessment of alternative solutions. From this point on, the process is similar to that required by performance-based codes.

Fire Behaviour
When considering issues of structural stability and life safety, it is important to understand that the greatest risk to the structure and its occupants comes from a fire that develops inside the building (a so-called 'compartment fire') rather than from a fire that occurs outside. In building code parlance, the word 'compartment' carries a specific meaning; that of an interior space or series of connected spaces that is separated from other such compartments in the building by fire-rated floors and walls. To appreciate the strategies that are needed to minimize the impacts of a compartment fire on the building and its occupants, it is helpful to understand how such a fire typically begins, and how it behaves as it develops.

Building codes can only regulate the materials used for the structure and finishes of a building, and not those that may be present in the furniture and fittings. Generally, it is the furnishings or 'contents' that present the greatest risk, and are the starting points for building fires. To start a fire, three things must be present simultaneously: fuel, oxygen and a source of ignition. Fire is an exothermic reaction in which oxygen and fuel are consumed, and heat (together with by-products such as smoke) is produced.

A fire will begin as an isolated phenomenon, but will grow in intensity and spread as it consumes the combustible contents and any exposed combustible structural elements of the compartment. Smoke will rise and spread across the ceiling, then down the walls while the temperature continues to rise. When the temperature of the smoke layer reaches approximately 600°C, the radiant heat emanating from it will cause most of the combustible objects below it to ignite. This almost instantaneous transition of the fire from localized to all-engulfing is called 'flashover'. In general, it is the availability of fuel that governs the development of a fire in the early stages and the supply of oxygen that determines its behaviour after the flashover.

Objectives of Fire Design
The most fundamental objective of fire design is to maintain structural stability and support the required loads during a fire event, such that the building will not collapse prematurely either during egress or

during the intervention of firefighters. Next in importance is life safety within floor areas or compartments of the building. This requires the implementation of measures to restrict both the development of a fire within the compartment in which it started, and the spread of heat or flames from that compartment to other areas of the building.

Typically, fire code engineering addresses these objectives using a combination of 'passive' and 'active' strategies. Passive strategies can be understood as encompassing such physical building attributes as material specification, fuel load, spatial compartmentation, and the number and location of fire exits and firefighting access points. Active strategies include fire alarms, heat and smoke detectors, automatic sprinkler and smoke venting systems, back-up generators and dedicated firefighting elevators.

While each of these measures, if implemented in an additive way, may be seen as providing incremental improvements in fire protection, they should rather be seen as an integrated suite of approaches (not all of which may be needed in every case) whose combined impact should ideally be evaluated using fire simulation modelling software.

Fire Simulation Modelling

A virtual three-dimensional fire model can be constructed to evaluate the effects of multiple variables, including the size and starting point of a fire, the degree of compartmentation, design details and materials used for fire separations and, in the case of Tall Wood buildings, the area and location of exposed wood surfaces. It is then possible to compare the results with those of entirely non-combustible buildings. The sophistication of these simulations is increasingly seen as providing a more accurate representation of real fire scenarios than the more formulaic 'time and temperature' approach that forms the baseline in prescriptive codes.

To ensure the success of a simulation-based approach, it is essential that the project stakeholders (design team, client, the authority having jurisdiction and the local fire department) work together with a fire engineer from the outset to develop a mutually agreeable fire protection methodology that respects the 'comfort zone' of all participants prior to proceeding with the detailed modelling analysis. This is important whatever structural material is being used, but particularly so for any project wishing to push the boundaries of wood construction.

Wood and Fire

The predictable performance of massive wood elements in fire is due to a combination of factors. First, the heat of the flames drives any free moisture in the wood toward the centre of the section, making it less susceptible to fire. At the same time, the charring of the surface creates an impervious insulating layer that protects the unburned interior of the wood, both from the heat of the fire and from the supply of oxygen necessary to sustain combustion. The conclusion to be drawn from the empirical evidence, as well as from simulation modelling, is that mass timber elements, even if exposed within a building do not make a substantial contribution to the overall fire load.

Fire Protection Options

Notwithstanding these conclusions, the approach to fire design may vary according to the preferences of the authority having jurisdiction, the local fire department or the client. Any one of these entities may consider that a particular design solution represents a greater level of risk, and hence liability, than they are prepared to take on.

Full Encapsulation

Faced with an unfamiliar building technology, these same entities may choose to take the most conservative route, and fully encapsulate the wood elements of the building in fire-resistant material, such as gypsum wallboard. This solution relies on the tried and tested approach that has commonly been used for steel or other 'unprotected' structures when fire resistance is required.

The Forte Building in Melbourne, Australia, 2012, by Andrew Nieland/Lend Lease Corporation, is an example of encapsulated construction in which the required fire resistance is achieved by covering the CLT structural elements with gypsum wallboard.

By following the same strategy for all other aspects of fire protection, it is possible to design a Tall Wood building that meets all the requirements for a non-combustible building of the same height – the only difference being that the structure itself is made from massive timber. This is the approach taken for projects such as Murray Grove in England [ill. p. 24] and Via Cenni in Italy [pp. 76–81].

Partial Encapsulation
A less conservative approach is that of partial encapsulation, where some of the massive timber elements are left exposed within the building. In terms of the hierarchy of risk, the structure itself is considered to be the most critical aspect of the fire protection effort, so in a partially encapsulated situation the structure would most likely remain concealed. Ceilings are the next most critical element, as this is where the smoke layer accumulates and heat builds up. Walls represent the area of least risk and are the most likely to remain exposed.

These general rules are open to interpretation and negotiation on a case by case basis, as seen in the Earth Sciences Building in Vancouver, Canada [ill. p. 44; see also pp. 102–107]. Here the glulam post-and-beam frame is exposed, but the soffits of the LSL composite floors are encapsulated in gypsum wallboard.

One secondary consideration of encapsulation is whether the fireproof material is installed tight to the structural elements, or whether it is secured to battens (in the case of a wall) or suspended (in the case of a ceiling) to create a void for service runs. In either case, additional measures such as mineral wool insulation or sprinklers may be required in the void to protect against the spread of fire or smoke.

Non-Encapsulated Construction
The third approach to fire protection is to leave as much wood as possible exposed, and to use fire simulation modelling and calculations to demonstrate compliance with all relevant performance criteria. This was the approach used on the Wood Innovation and Design Centre in Canada [ill. p. 43 and pp. 124–133] and the Woodcube in Germany [pp. 82–93].

Rather than protecting the wood structure from exposure to fire by covering it with non-combustible material, the wood is left exposed and fire resistance is achieved by calculating the depth of the 'sacrificial' layer of wood required to protect the structural section from fire damage. This thickness is based on the charring rate of around 40mm per hour, which varies somewhat depending on the wood species. For one-hour fire resistance all exposed surfaces of structural members would require an additional 40mm of timber that is allowed to char and so protects the structural section from damage.

In non-encapsulated construction, the most vulnerable part of the system in case of a fire is in fact the steel connectors between massive timber elements. All connectors must therefore be set into and covered by the timber, or protected from fire in some other way.

In the Wood Innovation and Design Centre in Prince George, British Columbia, fire protection is achieved using the charring method. Structural posts, beams and panels are oversized, creating a 'sacrificial layer' around the structural section that protects it from fire for the prescribed period. This permits the beauty of the structural members to be seen and appreciated.

Changing Attitudes to Fire Protection

While testing and simulation have confirmed that massive wood elements behave in a consistent and predictable manner when exposed to fire, it is worth remembering that we are still in the first phase of development for Tall Wood buildings. Research projects conducted in both North America and Europe have indicated that buildings in excess of 40 storeys are structurally feasible, but it is likely that these heights will be reached incrementally. However, as familiarity with Tall Wood construction increases, we will see the development of taller buildings, guided by greater confidence in non-traditional methods of fire protection.

ACOUSTIC PERFORMANCE

The acoustic performance of buildings has a significant role to play in occupant satisfaction, not just in performance spaces, but in residential and commercial environments as well.

In general, the acoustic performance of a space is determined by the level of background noise, the degree of sound isolation between adjacent spaces and from the exterior, and the acoustics of the room itself (which determines reverberation time and the intelligibility of speech). These acoustic parameters are controlled by the design and construction of enclosing elements, the sound attenuation of unwanted noise sources from outside the space and the appropriate specification and location of room finishes.

In contemporary high-performance buildings, passive design strategies can potentially conflict with the requirements of acoustic design. Multi-storey volumes that promote passive ventilation, or open plan spaces that improve the penetration of daylight can greatly increase the level of ambient noise, while the exposure

The Earth Sciences Building, in Vancouver, British Columbia, is an example of partial encapsulation in which the underside of the floors are protected with gypsum wallboard, while the posts and beams are left exposed.

of hard, dense materials for radiant heating and cooling can increase reverberation times and compromise speech intelligibility. These more qualitative aspects of acoustic design are not regulated by building codes that concern themselves mainly with sound isolation. For this reason, although important to occupant comfort, they are not dealt with in detail in this book.

Characteristics of Sound
Sound is a form of mechanical energy transmitted by vibration of the molecules of whatever medium the sound is passing through, air, water or building elements for example. A particular sound is defined by its:

- Frequency or pitch (measured in cycles per second or Hertz)
- Wavelength (measured in metres) and
- Amplitude or loudness (measured in decibels).

The range of hearing for a healthy child is approximately 20–20,000Hz, but may diminish in middle age to 70–14,000Hz. Human sensitivity to the frequency of sound is not consistent throughout this range, being greatest around 2500Hz. For the purposes of noise control, acousticians divide the sound spectrum into 16 equal intervals of one third octave each, and noise control standards focus on a range of 100–3150Hz (Europe) or 125–4000Hz (North America).

Sound Transmission in Buildings
In buildings sound is transmitted either through the air (airborne sound) or through the solid components of a spatial enclosure or building element (structure-borne sound). Airborne sound includes speech, music and other ambient noise from within or outside the building and is transmitted through the main partitions that separate spaces. Structure-borne sound (most critical-

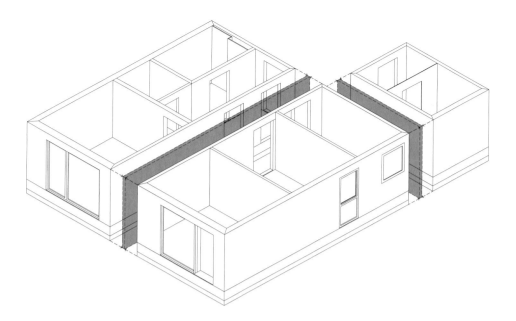

Treet in Bergen, Norway, uses volumetric prefabrication, in which the void between the walls of adjacent modular units is filled with acoustic insulation, reducing sound transmission between apartments.

ly transferred through floors or ceilings) can be the result of footsteps, the dropping of objects or the vibration of mechanical equipment in direct contact with the floor. Structure-borne sound is the result of vibrating surfaces radiating sound and, in many cases, can travel very efficiently in a structure.

In addition to these two modes of direct sound transmission, flanking sound is sound that is transmitted from one space to another by an indirect route, in much the same way as water will seep through the smallest of cracks in an otherwise sealed container. Flanking sound can travel via both airborne and structure-borne transmission paths.

Measuring Airborne Sound Transmission
Although the methods of measurement are similar in Europe and North America, different terms are used to quantify the reduction in intensity of airborne sound from one side of a building element to the other. In Europe, the term used is Sound Reduction Index (SRI), whereas in North America the term used is Sound Transmission Class (STC).

Testing of the element is carried out in a laboratory. Sound measurements are taken on both sides of the building element at a number of standard frequencies as noted above. The relative differences in sound pressure level between the source side and the receiving side are given a weighting according to their importance on the human auditory spectrum. These figures are then averaged and a single SRI rating calculated. This rating is expressed in decibels (dB).

Since the ratings are based on laboratory testing where ideal conditions exist, actual in-field tested values typically range between 3–5dB lower than those listed from lab testing. Such differences are a result of non-ideal conditions, potential construction deficiencies and other flanking paths that may limit the sound isolation performance of a partition.

Measuring Impact Sound Transmission
As with airborne sound, Europe and North America use different terms to quantify the transmission of impact sound. The term used in europe is impact sound insulation (ISI), whereas in North America, the equivalent rating is referred to as impact insulation class (IIC). Impact sound transmission is an important consideration in multi-storey buildings, as it quantifies the ability of a floor/ceiling assembly to reduce the transmission of impact noise from footsteps or the dropping of objects.

Both ISI and IIC ratings are based on test data obtained in accordance with the appropriate standard using a tapping machine. This is a device consisting of a series of five hammers that deliver blows of a given force at a prescribed rate. As with airborne sound transmission tests, measurements are taken on both sides of the building element being tested, and thus a value for impact sound transmission can be determined.

Sound Isolation Options

For optimal acoustic performance, it is important that both airborne sound and impact sound transmission are addressed in the design of floor/ceiling and wall assemblies. However, the strategies used to address these two forms of sound transmission can be quite different. The mass of a floor/ceiling or wall plays a significant role in the control of both airborne and impact sound. Beyond this common factor, however, noise reduction strategies diverge.

Airborne sound can be further attenuated by the provision of acoustic insulation – most often in the form of fibreglass or mineral fibre matting located in the cavity between finish and structure, or inside a stud cavity in frame construction. The structure of the matting is like a labyrinth, and sound waves bounce repeatedly off the fibres, converting their acoustic energy into heat energy.

On the other hand, the reduction of impact sound is achieved by breaking the physical continuity of the assembly that would otherwise provide a direct path for the transmission of vibration from one side to the other. Control of flanking sound relies on careful detailing of the junctions between the different elements of the enclosure, and at penetrations (such as ducts, pipes and wires) through these elements.

In multi-family residential buildings most North American codes require an STC rating of 50 and only provide a recommendation for IIC ratings of 55 corresponding to a speech sound reduction of approximately 50–55dB from one side of the floor/ceiling or wall assembly to the other.

Testing for massive wood floor/ceiling and wall systems is most advanced in Europe, where CLT-based systems in particular have been in use for a decade or more. The most comprehensive data comes from the French Institute of Technology for Forest-Based and Furniture Sectors (FCBA) located in Bordeaux. Testing undertaken by FCBA in collaboration with FP Innovations established that a standard five-layer CLT panel has an STC rating of 39 and an IIC rating of 24. For floor/ceiling assemblies, the introduction of a suspended (or independently supported) ceiling, together with other measures, can bring these values up to STC 60 and IIC 59 – both exceeding the standards required by the North American code[1].

Wall Assemblies

For wall assemblies, some Tall Wood buildings use CLT or other massive timber panels for exterior walls, but revert to light wood framing for partitions between apartment units where maximum sound attenuation is required. Most often, two frame walls are used in parallel with a small gap left between them to break the physical continuity of the assembly and hence reduce sound transmission. The outside face of each wall is typically lined with two layers of gypsum wallboard to increase the mass of the partition, and the interior cavities are filled with fibreglass or other acoustic insulation. In some situations, a discontinuity can also be introduced between floor panels at this point, further enhancing acoustic performance if the gap is filled with fire-resistant caulking. This approach was first taken in a Tall Wood building at the previously noted Limnologen project in Sweden [ill. p. 24 right]. Other common partition designs include single-panel CLT walls with gypsum wallboard fastened either to furring strips or resilient channels on one or both sides. The voids can be filled with acoustic insulation to further improve sound attenuation, and can also be used to run conduit or other services. This is the method that was used at Bridport House in London [pp. 64–69].

Partitions can also be constructed using two thinner CLT panels separated by a gap filled with acoustic insulation, and either left exposed or finished with gypsum wallboard as appropriate. However, the size of the air gap can also play a significant role in determining the sound transmission of a partition. Typically, a tradeoff exists between the mass of the wall assembly and the size of the airspace dividing the two wall finishes. In the event where a large airspace is not practically possible, a smaller airspace can be a good alternative but may require providing heavier wallboards.

Floor/Ceiling Assemblies
The design of floor/ceiling assemblies can also vary considerably, with the basic CLT or other massive timber panel being finished with an absorbent or resilient floor covering such as carpet or rubber. However, it is most effective to place the absorbent material in a cavity between the underside of the floor and the ceiling below. If space permits, and this ceiling can be independently supported, this maximizes the acoustic performance. This kind of floor/ceiling design is often implemented in Europe and was used, for instance, in the Strandparken Hus B project in Sundbyberg, Sweden [pp. 70–75].

By its very nature, volumetric prefabrication results in both floor/ceiling and wall assemblies that have two structural components independent of one another. This is because each volumetric unit has its own wall/ floor and ceiling assemblies and thus, when the units are brought together, there is generally a void between them that can be filled with acoustic insulation. Projects that employ this method of construction, such as Treet [ill. p. 45 top; see also pp. 158–163] and the Puukuokka Housing Block, in Jyväskylä, Finland [pp. 94–99] have made superior acoustic performance an inherent part of their systematized approach.

If there is insufficient depth available for an independently supported ceiling, resilient channels can be installed on the underside of the floor panels, with two layers of gypsum wallboard attached to them. The resilient channels are an extruded metal profile that acts as a 'spring' to dampen the vibration that would otherwise generate sound waves into the space below. Although the channel profile may be as little as 25mm deep, it nevertheless is worthwhile filling the space thus created with acoustic matting.

Design Variables and Synergies
The detailed design of floor/ceiling and wall assemblies will vary with a number of factors including: the available depth or thickness; the noise sensitivity of the space in question relative to adjacent program areas; whether the assembly in question has a fire resistance requirement; whether or not a concrete floor with radiant heat is being installed; what floor finishes are being specified; and the project budget.

As noted previously, acoustic requirements may conflict with other aspects of building performance, and therefore the design strategy must address multiple issues at once. For instance, for floor/ceiling assemblies, soft or resilient floor finishes such as carpet or rubber will decrease impact sound transmission and improve thermal insulation, but may at the same time compromise the performance of a radiant floor heating system. In all cases, an acoustical engineer's involvement at the early stages of a project is critical in ensuring the success of a wood building, especially as massive timber structures (often referred to as 'mass timber') become more common.

Where gypsum wallboard is mounted on resilient channels or furring strips on an interior partition or the underside of a floor/ceiling assembly, the resulting cavity can accommodate running services; it may also form an important part of an encapsulation strategy for structural fire resistance. Acoustic insulation may also double effectively as thermal insulation – as the mineral fibre matting does above and below the recessed balconies in the Puukuokka Housing Block in Finland. Poor acoustic performance is one of the most common complaints raised by the occupants of multi-family residential buildings in particular. Originally considered a potential weakness of Tall Wood buildings, ongoing research and testing of an increasing number of completed projects, has demonstrated that these buildings can easily meet the noise reduction requirements of current building codes. It is worth noting that occupant surveys conducted in the Limnologen project have recorded only one complaint about acoustic performance since the buildings were occupied in 2009.

THERMAL PERFORMANCE

The building enclosure acts as an environmental separator between inside and outside. Its primary function is to mitigate or harness the environmental forces acting upon it, and to maintain a comfortable thermal, visual and acoustic environment within the building. The factors that most affect the performance of a building enclosure, and ultimately the durability of the building itself are: the selection of materials, which must be designed for the required service life as well as be compatible with one another when incorporated into an assembly; the detailing of those assemblies to control thermal bridging, air, vapour and moisture movement; and quality control over fabrication and construction processes to ensure that the integrity of the enclosure is maintained over the service life of the building.

Building Enclosures for Tall Wood Structures

For Tall Wood structures, the design of the building enclosure must also take into consideration the unique properties of the material. This chiefly concerns its potential for damage from prolonged exposure to water, and the short- and long-term shrinkage that may occur as a result of structural loads or changes in moisture content.

While the building structure will be designed to minimize shrinkage and differential movement, the detailing of the enclosure must nonetheless accommodate any anticipated movement (which may vary considerably from the bottom to the top of the building), and also facilitate the drying of any moisture that might infiltrate the assembly. Weather protection of wood elements during construction is a critical component in quality assurance.

By definition, low-energy buildings must include high levels of insulation throughout the building enclosure. This results in an exceptionally steep temperature gradient across the roof or wall section between inside and outside. This in turn requires rigorous design and precise construction of the building enclosure to provide sufficient insulation, control thermal bridging, moisture and air movement, and to avoid condensation and mould growth.

Insulation

Insulation is only one of many components that make up the building envelope, although arguably it is the most important in terms of energy conservation and thermal comfort. The effectiveness of insulation to resist the flow of heat from one face of the material to the other is referred to as its thermal resistance, expressed as 'R-value'. The higher the R-value, the better the level of insulation provided. The reciprocal of an R-value is a U-factor, which is a measurement not of thermal resistance, but of thermal conductance. Thus, the more effective the insulation, the lower its U-factor will be. When assessing the thermal performance of building envelope components, it is more common in North America to refer to R-values while in Europe the reference to U-factors is typical.

Without exception, thermal insulation has a positive environmental impact because it reduces the amount of operating energy a building will require over its service life. However, the ecological footprint of the material itself is also a consideration, although this may be hard to define. This impact will depend on a variety of factors, including its method of extraction, processing and fabrication.

The most environmentally benign insulation materials in common use are fibreglass, mineral wool (based on rock, glass, ceramic or steel slag, which are often chosen for their fire resistance), and wood fibre or cellulose fibre, which are available as rigid boards or in loose and spray-applied form.

Thermal insulation can also perform other functions such as fire resistance, humidity control and/or noise reduction. All insulation materials have their own strengths and weaknesses, and these should be evaluated against the design criteria. Both wood fibre and cellulose fibre insulation are more sensitive to water exposure than their mineral fibre counterparts. However, if this exposure can be closely controlled, the hygroscopic nature of these materials can contribute

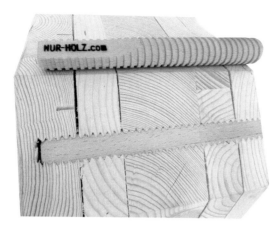

Section through the exterior wall of the Woodcube in Hamburg, Germany. The wall uses structural CLT panels fastened with wooden dowels, wood fibre and cellulose insulation and wood cladding, a demonstration that wood products can fulfil all the functional requirements for the building envelope.

to humidity stabilization, making them particularly suited to vapour-open construction.

Thermal resistance values for equivalent thicknesses of insulation vary somewhat from one material to another, with mineral wool and fibreglass typically being slightly better insulators than cellulose fibre and wood fibre. However, this minor difference in thermal performance may be outweighed by other design considerations, such as greater thermal mass (which can contribute to temperature stabilization), fire resistance or acoustic performance.

Vapour Retarders

Vapour retarders are used to control the diffusion of water vapour through the building envelope, and prevent vapour from condensing on colder surfaces as it migrates through an assembly. Vapour retarders are most important in cold climates in which the need for heating (rather than cooling) predominates. They are installed on the warm (interior) side of the insulation in most wall and roof assemblies, and typically consist of a coating, a membrane, boards or other rigid materials.

The rate at which vapour diffuses through a material is referred to as permeance, and is measured in perms. The values of a metric perm and a US perm are different,[2] but the principles of design remain the same. The relative vapour permeance of materials is generally classified by the descriptors: vapour-impermeable, vapour-semi permeable and vapour-permeable. It is important to understand the relative vapour permeance of all the material layers making up the building enclosure, in order to successfully design vapour-open assemblies. The sequence of insulation layers should be increasingly more vapour-permeable as one moves from the inside to the outside of the building enclosure.

European practice, as seen in the Woodcube [ill. p. 49 above; see also pp. 82–93], is to choose a layer at or close to the interior face of the primary wall assembly, to act as a vapour retarder. This could be a layer of painted gypsum wallboard, plywood, OSB (oriented strand board) or an exposed CLT (or other massive timber) panel. Working outward from this interior face, the wall includes additional layers of insulating material that have incrementally greater vapour permeance. In the event that moisture penetrates the interior of the wall assembly, or interstitial condensation occurs, this enables it to dry out naturally, with the moisture migrating from inside to outside

Air Barriers

Air barriers can be used anywhere in a building envelope assembly to stop the movement of air into` or out of the conditioned space and hence control heat loss or gain as well as moisture transfer. The rate at which air will pass through an air barrier will depend on the pressure difference from one side to the other. In service, this will be affected by mechanical pressure within the building, wind direction and speed (which can create high- or low-pressure areas adjacent to the exterior surface of the building), and the temperature difference between the inside and outside of the building.

Whereas air permeance is the amount of air that permeates through an air barrier or other material, air leakage is the quantity of air that passes through holes or gaps. Even small openings can severely compromise the performance of an air barrier, so achieving and maintaining continuity in the barrier is crucial. Water vapour can also be transported by air movement.

Air barriers can be mechanically fastened building wraps, self-adhered membranes, fluidly or spray-applied materials, rigid sheathing products such as plywood or gypsum wallboard, or any other layer that resists the passage of air. (Note that materials such as synthetic building wraps are vapour-permeable, even though they may function as an air barrier.)

An air barrier can be positioned at any point in the assembly, whether at the inside face, outside face or somewhere in between. The key concern is that it must be continuous, with lapped joints if it is a film or membrane, sealed joints if it is of panel construction – and all penetrations (whether pipes, ducts, windows or doors) must also be sealed to prevent air leakage.

Water-Resistive Barriers

A water-resistive barrier is a layer positioned within the wall assembly to protect vulnerable components from damage caused by water penetrating the assembly from the outside. In conjunction with surface water control, water shedding surfaces, flashings and other details, water-resistive barriers redirect water to the outside, and away from the building.

The first line of defence is often a rainscreen cladding system, in which the cladding is fastened to vertical battens mounted on the exterior face of the wall assembly. The battens create a series of vertical cavities that are vented top and bottom (or at every floor level). Any water that finds its way past the cladding and into the cavity, runs down the water barrier to the next flashing where it is redirected to the outside.

Water-resistive barriers can be mechanically fastened building wraps, fluidly applied membranes, cellular plastic or self-adhered membranes. As with air barriers, the detailing of water barriers and their various flashings, caps and seals is of particular importance in wood construction, because prolonged exposure to moisture may cause fungus or mould, or create conditions conducive to insect attack.

Moisture Control

Ensuring that the presence of moisture in the building envelope remains at an acceptable level begins with the protection of materials during transportation, storage and installation. The moisture content of the wood components should not exceed 19%. Testing may be required to confirm that moisture content is at an acceptable level prior to the installation of interior finishes.

Control of moisture in roof assemblies prior to and during installation is of critical importance, as once a roof assembly gets wet, it is extremely difficult and time-consuming to dry it out. In Scandinavia, protection of the wood structure during construction is a standard practice, using either a tent mounted on self-extending scaffolding, as was the case at Limnologen [ill. p. 24 right] and Strandparken Hus B [pp. 70–75], or a temporary removable roof, as at the Puukuokka Housing Block [pp. 94–99]. In Britain and North America, weather protection (beyond the factory installation of membranes on roof panels and the wrapping of components during transportation) tends to be in response to adverse weather conditions, rather than a pre-emptive preventative measure.

Maintaining the desired moisture content in service depends on the effectiveness of the design and detailing strategies in controlling air, water and vapour movement. With a carefully detailed enclosure, the equilibrium moisture content of wood within the building will remain below 19% – and in most situations will remain between 8 and 12%.

Thermal Bridging

The thermal performance of a building envelope depends not only on the continuity of the air barrier, but on the integrity of the insulation. In the solid portions of walls or roofs, thermally conductive components (such as those made from concrete or steel) should not penetrate the full depth of the insulation as they will create 'thermal bridges', where heat loss or condensation will occur.

Because of their superior thermal resistance it is possible for wood elements to penetrate the building envelope without significantly affecting its overall performance. For example, the CLT floor panels used in the Woodcube [ill. p. 49; see also pp. 82–93] cantilever 2.5 metres to create exterior balconies. However, the more common practice, as implemented at Strandparken Hus B [pp. 70–75] and Bridport House [pp. 64–69], is to maintain the integrity of the enclosure. Here the balcony structures do not penetrate the building envelope, being independent CLT panels, suspended by rods that are attached directly to the external wall structure (but do not penetrate the insulation). Window and door frames that penetrate the full depth of the exterior wall assembly must be 'thermally broken', with insulating material separating the various parts of the frame, or constructed from non-conductive material such as wood or fibreglass.

While individual high-performance wood frame windows (often with an exterior covering of aluminum) have been available in most jurisdictions for some time, high-performance European wood-framed curtain wall systems are a recent arrival in North America. These factory-prefabricated systems can provide an effective U-value of 0.125 (R-8) when fitted with argon-filled, insulated triple-glazed units.

The improved performance relative to traditional curtain wall systems is in part due to the substitution of wood mullions for aluminum ones, but also to the careful detailing of the multiple seals and thermal breaks within the assembly. A simulation conducted by AIR-INS, an independent testing agency in Montreal, Canada, concluded that this technology can be 30–60% more efficient than other North American curtain wall options. Similarly, infrared photography of timber-framed façade installations reveals more consistent surface temperatures with greatly reduced thermal bridging at framing members.

Site-assembled wood curtain wall systems can also achieve superior performance relative to traditional aluminum systems. The site-built system installed at the Wood Innovation and Design Centre in Canada [pp. 124–133], which combines LVL structural mullions with triple-glazed argon-filled, insulated units, achieves an effective U-value of 0.2 (R-5), which is approximately 40% better than that of an equivalent site-built aluminum system.

CONCLUSION

An appreciation of the unique properties of wood, and a comprehensive understanding of building physics is essential when incorporating wood into the design of a high-performance building enclosure. Temperature gradients, pressure differences, vapour migration and other environmental factors must be taken into consideration when selecting materials and designing details. Equally important, precise fabrication and protection from moisture during construction are key to the successful realization of effective, reliable and durable building enclosures.

REFERENCES

1   FP Innovations (2009). Acoustic Performance Handbook. Retrieved from http://www.woodusematrix.com/database/rte/files/ CLT-Acoustic%20Performance.pdf

2   The US perm is defined as 1 grain of water vapour per hour, per square foot, per inch of mercury, whereas the base normal SI (metric) perm is 1 kilogram per second per square meter per pascal.

DESIGN AND CONSTRUCTION

Speaking at the Third International Congress on Construction History in 2009, Professor Ryan E. Smith, Director of the Center for Integrated Design and Construction at the University of Utah, observed that 'technology is an outgrowth of social needs and desires, not the other way around.'[1] This statement goes some way to explaining why approaches to the construction of buildings have varied considerably from region to region around the world, a phenomenon due in part to differences in geography, demographics, economics and the availability of materials and labour. However, the global trend towards higher-quality, higher-performance buildings that last longer and consume less energy is catalyzing a cultural convergence. This is particularly evident in the design and construction of Tall Wood buildings, where off-site construction has

demonstrated its advantages in delivering precise, high-quality components and assemblies that meet design expectations and promise an extended service life. This is no surprise in Europe, where off-site construction has been associated with both economy and quality, dating back to the much admired prefabricated social housing projects of Ernst May in 1920s Germany. By contrast, North America is only now beginning to recognize the virtues of prefabrication, this approach to construction having long been associated with the sub-standard modular homes that dominate the continent's many trailer parks.

OFF-SITE AND ON-SITE CONSTRUCTION

When the majority of the building work takes place in the controlled environment of a factory or production plant, it is much easier to achieve high-quality workmanship, and to provide the required assurances of performance. Generally a factory provides a safer working environment, eliminating the vagaries of weather, the likelihood of workplace injuries from tripping or falling, and, by bringing operations to bench level, can eliminate the need for work to be done overhead or in cramped spaces.

In addition, the predictability of factory production can contribute to more accurate estimations of cost and time. Particularly when production is multi-station or takes place on an assembly line, this advantage can be extended to include the work of multiple trades. This means that electrical, mechanical and other systems can be integrated into prefabricated components that require only 'plug-and-play' connections on site. The potential impact on site construction times relative to traditional project delivery methods is significant. Reductions of 50–80% are consistently realized, and this can make a considerable difference to the project costs, as well as greatly reducing the disruption to the neighbourhood around the construction site – a particular advantage in urban areas.

With an increasing emphasis on urban redevelopment and densification, building sites tend to be more compact and have smaller (if any) areas available for the storage of materials. Prefabrication can address this problem by facilitating just-in-time delivery of components, so that no on-site inventory is required, and installation is immediate.

Off-Site Construction of Tall Wood Buildings

When building in wood, the advantages of off-site construction are even more pronounced. In addition to the – often prefabricated – structural members, such as beams and columns, or building elements such as walls, floors and roofs, the lightness of wood also makes possible the prefabrication of volumetric components.

Fully enclosed modular units can be fabricated, complete with all finishes and fittings – a technique that reduces the time required for on-site construction to an absolute minimum. This technology was employed both at Treet [pp. 158–163] and at the Puukuokka Housing Block [pp. 94–99]. Depending on the size of these units, it may still be possible to lift them into place using only a truck-mounted crane.

As noted above, shorter on-site construction times mean a reduced volume of construction-related traffic, and less disruption to the surrounding neighbourhood. When building in wood, there is also a reduction in construction noise (as most operations require only hand-held power tools) as well as less construction-related dust and debris.

Bringing construction into the factory is also an important part of weather protection, which is more critical for wood than for most other materials. With components wrapped during transportation and delivered on a just-in-time schedule, it is possible to limit the exposure to rain and other sources of moisture. In addition, if the fabrication of building elements such as roofs and exterior walls includes the installation of membranes, cladding or other finishes, the possibility for water damage is further reduced.

Prefabrication has already proven its effectiveness in the delivery of projects with highly repetitive programs, one notable example being the 93-bedroom Ammerwald Hotel near Reutte, Austria, designed by Oskar Leo Kaufmann and Albert Rüf, and completed in 2009 [ill. p. 54 and 55].

The hotel, commissioned by BMW as a mountain retreat for its employees, comprises three storeys of bedrooms constructed in CLT, on top of a two-storey concrete podium that accommodates the public areas of the facility. The CLT components were designed as a 'kit of parts' that would fit snugly into standard shipping containers. This facilitated efficient truck transportation to the remote site, with installation of all the wood components taking less than ten days.

A more recent example is the eight-storey student residence building at the University of East Anglia in Norwich, England, designed by LSI Architects and completed in 2013. The complex contains 230 student apartments, each with an en-suite bathroom, and was

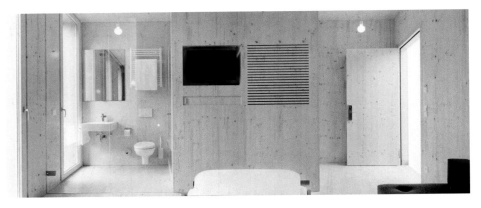

The Ammerwald Hotel, located near Reutte, Austria, 2009, by Oskar Leo Kaufmann and Albert Rüf, was designed using a modular system that enabled each hotel suite to be fully prefabricated and finished in a workshop (including bathroom fixtures) before being shipped to site.

constructed as a load-bearing 'platform' structure using CLT wall and floor panels. The repetitive wood structure was erected in only 12 weeks, including installation of modular bathrooms for each unit [ill. p.56].

Market Transformation

In many developed countries, where the shortage of quality affordable housing has become more acute over the last two decades, modular prefabrication offers hope of a solution. In the United Kingdom, where the increase in house prices has far outstripped the increase in household incomes, it is estimated that by 2025, one quarter of 20–49 year olds will require affordable rental housing.

As currently structured, the UK housing industry is only capable of delivering half of the 250,000 new housing units required each year. However in 2016, Legal & General, a major London-based financial services company, announced its intention to enter the rental housing market, and plans to open the country's largest modular housing factory. The factory will fabricate volumetric CLT townhouse and apartment units, the latter to be used for buildings of up to 20 storeys. The focus will be suburban and urban densification, with 3000 units in outer London currently in the planning phase.

INTEGRATED DESIGN

The design of today's sustainable buildings requires integral thinking, involving a spectrum of disciplines that, traditionally, were engaged individually or sequentially. Increasingly the areas of design expertise overlap, and the systems within a building perform multiple functions. For example, the size and placement of windows is no longer exclusively an architectural concern, as maximizing daylight and minimizing unwanted solar gain clearly have an impact on the design of electrical and mechanical systems. Bringing the required consultants together from the outset of a project maximizes the synergies that can be achieved in the design of a building, and minimizes the potential conflicts that might otherwise occur. Involving fabricators and contractors helps ensure that solutions are economical and readily constructible. This Integrated Design Process (IDP) enables alternative approaches to be evaluated at the schematic design stage, and allows for conflicts to be resolved during design development and for contract documents to reflect a building that has been proven in virtual models before any fabrication or construction begins. Such an approach is increasingly important to the success of any project, but even more so in the design of Tall Wood buildings.

Wood elements in a building can perform multiple functions and the input of numerous design consultants may be required to ensure that these potential synergies are capitalized upon. Among the more common examples of multi-functional elements that will require collaboration between disciplines are: structural wood members that, if sized appropriately, may provide structural fire resistance in addition to their basic load-carrying function; wood or wood fibre elements that may contribute to both thermal and acoustic performance; or engineered wood panels that may serve simultaneously as an architectural finish and part of the lateral system of the building. Among the less common examples to be found in this book is the detailed design of the wood rainscreen cladding on the Woodcube [pp. 82–93], where the coffered design and horizontal fire stopping combine to meet the intent of the local fire code.

The hotel was constructed in CLT on top of a two-storey concrete podium. The CLT components were designed as a 'kit of parts' transported by trucks to the remote site, with installation taking less than ten days.

The highly repetitive CLT structure of the eight-storey student residence at the University of East Anglia, in Norwich, England, by LSI Architects, was completed in 2013 in just 12 weeks.

Systems Integration

For reasons of economy, efficiency and indoor environmental quality, contemporary buildings use fewer finishes than was standard practice in the past. As a consequence, it is more common for structural elements to be left exposed, and this is most frequently the case when wood is the primary structural material. This in turn leads to services such as electrical conduit, sprinkler pipes and mechanical ductwork potentially being exposed in the occupied areas of the building. While it is relatively straightforward to accommodate vertical service risers into the core of commercial buildings, as has been done at both the Wood Innovation and Design Centre [pp. 124–133] and LCT One [pp. 142–151], it is much more difficult to distribute them horizontally.

The integration of these systems within the overall architectural expression is important to the success of the building and requires considerable coordination. The two-layer CLT floor system in the Wood Innovation and Design Centre uses a staggered lattice structure that permits services to be routed within the depth of the structural floor, and concealed from below by slatted wood panels. In LCT One, the composite concrete and glulam floor system works in conjunction with a raised floor system to accommodate concealed service runs.

In residential buildings, the distribution of electrical and plumbing systems may be decentralized, reflecting the greater compartmentation of the building program. The Woodcube [pp. 82–93] and the Puukuokka Housing Block [pp. 94–99] to a large degree use the same approach, the former distributing multiple service risers around the perimeter of the building; the latter positioning them along the central corridor. Wall finishes can be used selectively, mounted on continuous battens to create a void in which conduit can be run, and suspended ceilings in kitchens and bathrooms conceal ducts for fans. In volumetric prefabrication, these spaces are included in 'wet' modules that are positioned adjacent to mechanical and electrical risers to shorten service runs. As noted in chapter 5, Building Performance, wherever services pass through fire separations, acoustic partitions or the exterior envelope of the building, sealing of openings is required to maintain the integrity of the separation.

CONCLUSION

Just as optimal design is dependent on an increased level of integration, so is optimal performance of buildings dependent on an increased quality of construction. It is important that all members of the design and construction team understand how their work interfaces with that of others. In this way, the realization of high-performance buildings becomes a collaborative effort, requiring a new level of cooperation between design professionals and contractors. The old paradigm, which often set these parties in opposition to one another, has no place in the emerging field of Tall Wood.

REFERENCES

1   Smith, Ryan E. (2009). Prefabrication: A Cultural History. University of Utah. Retrieved from http://www.bma.arch.unige.it/pdf/construction_history_2009/vol3/smith-ryan_vw_paper_layouted.pdf

TECHNOLOGY

The evolution of contemporary massive timber construction (often shortened to 'mass timber') is inextricably linked with the application of digital fabrication technology to components of architectural scale. This in turn has been made possible by the development of design software capable of modelling entire structures in three dimensions, and generating fully dimensioned fabrication drawings complete with tolerances, for each structural member and all other elements. These digital files can then be used to program computerized numerical controlled (CNC) machines that can cut, plane, drill and rout components of almost any size and shape. The accuracy of CNC machining also makes the integration of a new generation of high-strength proprietary connection systems possible.

CNC MANUFACTURING

While CNC fabrication lends itself to the creation of complex shapes, the principles behind the technology are quite straightforward. The term CNC simply refers to a manufacturing process in which the machining tool is instructed and controlled by a computer program. The process can be applied to any material, and was first used in the 1940s, to machine the increasingly complex aluminum parts required by the US aircraft industry.

The application of CNC technology to the manufacture of wood furniture dates to the 1970s, with the introduction of machines that could move with precision along a single axis to drill simple holes. Next came two-axis machines that could make a saw cut perpendicular to the initial path of travel, then three-axis machines that could move linearly in the X, Y and Z directions. Contemporary CNC machines can also perform operations that involve rotation about one or more of these axes, and can mill, rout and drill highly complex shapes. These operations may require both a moving table (upon which the component rests) and a mobile cutting head.

For Tall Wood buildings, CNC offers numerous advantages. By automating the production process, CNC manufacturing reduces the number of skilled workers required, and transfers work from the field to the factory. There it can be applied to the preparation of digital shop drawings and the programming of machinery. Increasingly, digital production appeals to the new generation of workers for whom interaction with technology is more stimulating than manual labour. CNC production also offers much greater precision than manual fabrication. Tolerances of +/–0.5mm or less are achievable, greatly reducing the magnitude and attendant effect of accumulated errors when multiple components are assembled on site. As discussed in chapter 5, Building Performance, this precision is particularly critical when dealing with buildings that have high-performance expectations.

Additionally, as changing the output of a CNC machine is simply a question of sending it new digital information, there can be considerable flexibility in how production schedules are organized. It is possible to manufacture a multitude of different components sequentially, with minimal downtime, meaning that suites of related components can be produced on a just-in-time basis, or multiple jobs can be run simultaneously. This flexibility in turn leads to greater efficiency and economy and more predictable production costs and schedules. CNC technology also facilitates the integration of new high-performance proprietary connection systems that enable the construction of larger, lighter and more efficient structures.

CONNECTION SYSTEMS

In a Tall Wood building, as in any other structure, connections are required to provide strength, stiffness, stability and ductility – resisting or dissipating the various forces to which the building is subjected. A connection should be considered as a 'system' that includes all the elements required to transfer load from one component of the structure to another, and ultimately to the ground.

Connection performance is particularly critical in relation to the extreme forces imposed by high winds or seismic events, as the collapse of buildings under such circumstances has often been attributed to the failure of connections. The taller the building, the higher the imposed loads: dead loads because of the extra weight of each additional storey; live loads because of the additional surface area presented to the wind, or the increased seismic forces that a heavier building will attract.

The connection systems used in the projects featured in this book have been designed to transfer loads from wood to wood, wood to steel and wood to concrete. They include: traditional techniques such as dowels and dovetails; fasteners such as nails and screws; hardware such as brackets, hangers, tie-rods and knife plates; and a variety of proprietary systems, some of which use epoxy or other adhesives. Concealed connectors are employed where the structure is exposed and a fire rating is required. As explained in chapter 5, Building Performance, pp. 39–41, the wood is used to cover the metal components of the connection and provide the required protection from heat.

In wood structures, connections of all types must take into consideration the natural characteristics of the material, such as its different strength parallel and perpendicular to grain, its cellular structure, and its response (through expansion and contraction) to changes in moisture content. Wood performs better when loaded parallel to grain, when multiple small connections are used to spread the load (rather than a smaller number of large connections), and when the material is dried to and kept at a moisture content between 8 and 15%. In addition to these considerations, massive timber elements are inherently stiff. In order to dissipate seismic and wind forces, ductility must be

At the Bullitt Center in Seattle, Washington, a steel connector was used between the top of one post and the base of the next. The same depth as the NLT floor panels, this spacer avoids cross grain material in the vertical section of the building, minimizing the effects of shrinkage.

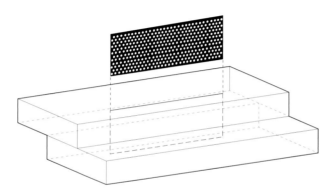

The Wood Innovation and Design Centre uses an innovative system of HSK mesh and epoxy adhesive to connect the upper and lower panels of CLT used in the floor and roof structures.

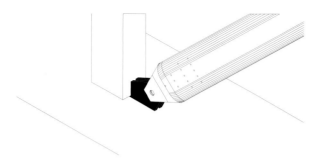

The steel knife plates and brackets that connect the chevron braces at the Earth Sciences Building in Vancouver, Canada, provide the ductility necessary to absorb and dissipate seismic forces.

designed into connections, usually through the intro-duction of steel.

LOAD TRANSFER

As explained in chapter 4, Structural Systems, p. 32, it is important to avoid cross grain material in the verti-cal section, to minimize the effects of shrinkage and avoid the possibility of crushing and deformation. A number of strategies serve to achieve this: direct end grain-to-end grain bearing of columns, as employed at the Wood Innovation and Design Centre [pp. 124–133] through the use of steel plate and dowel connectors [ill. p. 61 right]; the use of spacers or plugs inserted in the floor panels, as used at Via Cenni [pp. 76–81]; or castellated wall panels, as used at Bridport House [pp. 64–69]. Each of these approaches has particular implications for the connection hardware used.

In frame systems, the post-and-beam connections can be made in a variety of ways, including hardware in the form of 'buckets', as at the Bullitt Center [ill. p. 60 top; see also pp. 118–123]; concealed epoxy-based proprietary connectors, as at the Wood Innovation and Design Centre [ill. p. 60 centre] and LCT One [pp. 142–151]; or knife plates, as at Treet [pp. 158–163]. Alter-natively, wood-to-wood connections are possible, such as the custom-milled oval dowels used in the Tamedia Head Office [ill. p. 61 left; see also pp. 108–117], or the interior column detail on the Earth Sciences Building. Lateral forces can also be resisted in a variety of ways, including the use of cross bracing or shear walls con-nected together with floor and roof diaphragms. Shear walls are connected to the foundations with shear con-nectors and tie-down anchors. Cross bracing is used in Treet and chevron bracing in the Earth Sciences Build-ing [ill. p. 60 bottom; see also pp. 102–107], where in-ternal steel knife plates and dowels provide the re-quired ductility.

Internal and external shear walls are part of the later-al system in most load-bearing CLT structures, with Via Cenni having a particularly straightforward and pragmatic approach to seismic design. There, the walls are 'stitched' to the floors using closely spaced,

Precision CNC milled dowels are used to connect the post-and-beam frame in the Tamedia Head Office in Zurich, Switzerland. The oval cross section of the dowels prevents rotation, enabling the connection to resist lateral loads.

At the Wood Innovation and Design Centre in Prince George, British Columbia, steel rods are used to connect the superimposed columns. This end grain-to-end grain connection minimizes vertical shrinkage in the structure.

high-strength stainless steel screws inserted at opposing angles of 45° to the vertical – not unlike the toe-nailing technique used in light wood framing. The close spacing and inherent ductility of these proprietary screws is designed to dissipate seismic forces evenly throughout the structure. At Strandparken Hus B [pp. 70–75] steel rods running vertically through the CLT walls, tie the building from the uppermost floor to the slab of the concrete parking garage. Used in conjunction with shear walls, these tie rods improve lateral stability and resist uplift due to wind.

Floor diaphragms for lateral resistance can be created by connecting CLT or LVL panels together using lap joints or splines, or by adding plywood in a staggered pattern. Alternatively, a reinforced concrete topping cast on top of CLT or other floor panels can also create a diaphragm. Cree developed its own proprietary system to bolt together the precast wood/concrete composite panels in LCT One [pp. 142–151]. A wood/concrete composite floor system was used in the Earth Sciences Building [pp. 102–107]. Here strips of metal mesh are glued into saw cuts in the LSL floor panels, then cast into a concrete slab that is poured on top. In this system, the reinforced concrete topping and LSL panels act together to form a diaphragm. A similar epoxy-based system is employed in the all-wood floor structure of the Wood Innovation and Design Centre [pp. 124–133]. Here, the upper and lower panels of the double-layer CLT floor system (which run perpendicular to one another), are joined by metal

mesh strips epoxy-glued into saw kerfs at the points where the panels intersect.

CONCLUSION

While the vertical, lateral and other forces to which Tall Wood buildings are subjected are similar in character whatever their location, the methods used to resist these forces may well differ from region to region. The choice of connections forms part of an integrated approach to structural design that is influenced by material selection, performance requirements, the constraints of program, local construction practice and economics. From a technical perspective, realizing the full potential of Tall Wood structures depends to a great extent on the precision of digital design and fabrication, and the use of high-efficiency connection systems. As confidence grows among architects, engineers and most importantly clients and municipal authorities, a new generation of Tall Wood buildings is already being imagined.

PANEL SYSTEMS

Panel systems are those in which vertical and horizontal loads are carried by a series of regularly spaced solid wall panels arranged in two directions in plan. Most often made from CLT, these panels ideally have the same configuration and spacing on each floor of the building.

Because panel systems tend to result in cellular plan arrangements with limited flexibility for reconfiguration over the life of the building, they are generally better suited to residential programs, where occupant needs are fixed.

Nonetheless, architects and structural engineers can adapt these basic principles in various ways, some of which are illustrated in the following portfolio of projects:

– Bridport House uses CLT panels as transfer beams that enable the smaller structural grid of the upper floor apartments to be superimposed on the larger structural grid of the ground floor maisonettes.

– Strandparken Hus B is constructed using wall panels with a CLT core, but which are factory-fitted with doors and windows, insulation and exterior and interior finishes before being shipped to site.

– Via Cenni, built to stringent seismic codes, has a rigorous cellular construction with floor and wall panels stitched together with a large number of extra-long screws.

– The Woodcube increases interior spans with steel reinforcing beams, providing greater flexibility for internal reconfiguration.

– The Puukuokka Housing Block incorporates its load-bearing CLT panels into volumetric prefabricated units that are then stacked vertically on site.

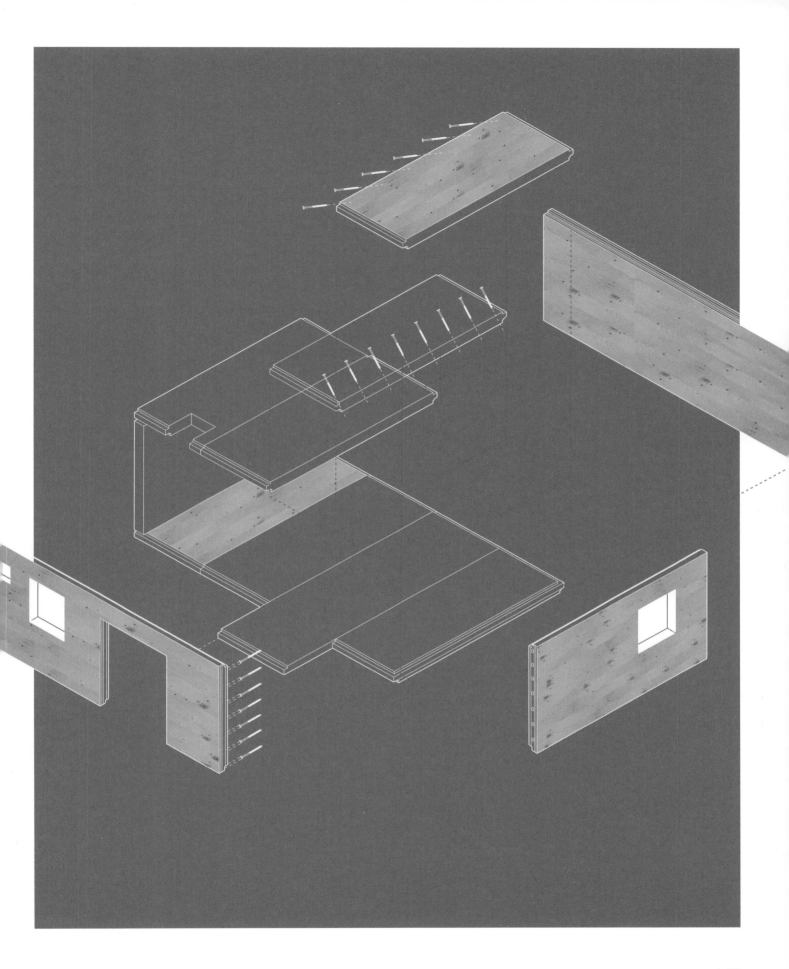

BRIDPORT HOUSE

London, England [Karakusevic Carson Architects]

2011	**Year**
The London Borough of Hackney	**Client**
Peter Brett Associates	**Structural Engineer**
Eurban	**Engineered Wood Fabricator**
Willmott Dixon	**Contractor**
Residential	**Program**

This social housing project refines the techniques of load-bearing CLT construction, improving its economy, efficiency and structural performance.

The building follows the changing angle of the property line and can be accessed from the street and the courtyard.

Completed in 2011, this social housing project was commissioned by the London Borough of Hackney, a leading public sector advocate for Tall Wood construction in the United Kingdom. It is the first of five phases in the redevelopment of the 1960s-era Colville Estate, a poorly planned and inward-looking estate consisting chiefly of medium-height linear blocks. Light in weight, quick and easy to erect, Bridport House illustrates many of the advantages prefabricated massive timber construction can offer in the densification of existing urban areas.

CONCEPT

Bridport House was the winning entry in a design competition for a housing project, to replace existing five-storey, 20-unit apartment buildings with one more than twice the size. The brief specified a tight two-year schedule from the start of design to the completion of construction, and a site with poor soil conditions traversed by a 2.5 metre diameter Victorian-era storm sewer presented another challenge.

This latter constraint dictated that any replacement building must not increase foundation loads by more than 15%. The solution was an eight-storey all-CLT structure with a concrete ground floor slab, supported on pile foundations. The 41-unit, 4020-square metre building includes two-storey ground level maisonettes, with individual access and internal staircases, and six storeys of one- to three-bedroom apartment units above. The upper floors are accessed via two double-height entrance lobbies.

The dark brick cladding gives the building a dignified character, unusual for a social housing project of this type, while the projecting balconies, suspended by tie rods directly from the CLT panels, animate the street façade.

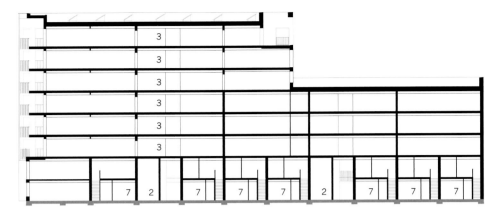

Section AA

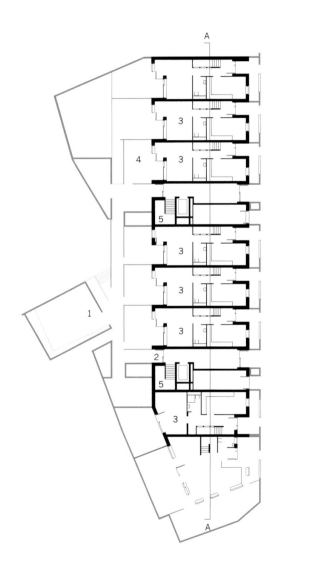

Ground floor plan

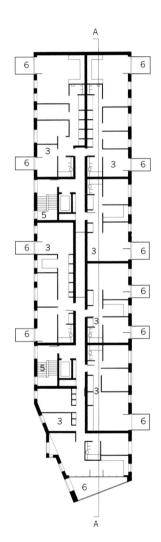

Typical floor plan

1 Outdoor area
2 Entrance area
3 Apartment
4 Personal outdoor area
5 Stairwell
6 Balcony
7 Two-storey residence

One of the apartments under construction

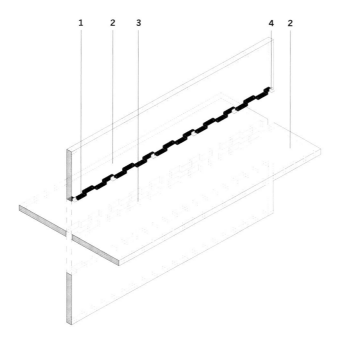

Axonometric drawing of CLT dovetail connections
1 Vertical CLT panels have dovetails cut into them. These cuts slip through corresponding cuts in the horizontal boards resulting in an end grain-to-end grain connection within the vertical walls. **2** CLT wall panels **3** Dovetails in the horizontal panels enable the vertical panels to bear on one another. **4** Metal brackets additionally secure the individual panels to one another.

CONSTRUCTION

The requirement to locate the larger maisonette units on the ground floor, and the smaller apartment units above, presented some structural challenges, as it was necessary to superimpose the structural grid for the apartments onto the structural grid for the maisonettes. This required the creation of a CLT transfer structure at second floor level, with the CLT wall elements acting as transfer beams spanning between the party walls of the maisonettes below. The transfer of vertical loads was accomplished using custom steel saddles.

Another structural challenge related to the height and construction method used for the building. The concerns were twofold: for one that in an eight-storey building the presence of cross grain CLT floor panels in the vertical section of the building might result in excessive shrinkage, and secondly that the superimposed loads might exacerbate the problem by crushing the floor panels.

The solution was to 'castellate' both floor and wall panels so that they could be connected in a dovetail fashion. The projections on the upper surface of each wall panel could thus be in contact with the lower surface of the panel above, creating an end grain bearing condition with sufficient load-carrying capacity. Wall panels vary in thickness from 100mm at the top of the building, to 160mm at the bottom – a response to the greater superimposed loads. At the same time, the projections on the floor panels form a connection with the cut-out portions of the wall panel, providing enough bearing surface to transfer dead and live loads into the cross walls and hence to the foundations.

Exterior view of two-storey unit on the ground floor

The lateral system for the building is a combination of cross walls in one direction, and a floor diaphragm that transfers loads into the CLT stair and elevator shafts in the other direction. This gives flexibility to the interior layout of apartments, permitting the interior walls to be of light metal stud construction, easily deconstructed and reconfigured if needed.

Demising walls between suites are CLT panels with battens, 50mm of acoustic insulation and two layers of gypsum wallboard on both sides. The floors have a sand and cement screed topping and two layers of gypsum wallboard fastened to the soffit. In addition, there is a suspended ceiling with one layer of gypsum wallboard and 50mm of acoustic insulation. These measures provide approximately 60dB of sound reduction, considerably more than that required by code.

Fire protection of the structure is provided through encapsulation, with the building requiring no sprinklers, but being fitted with a smoke alarm system for

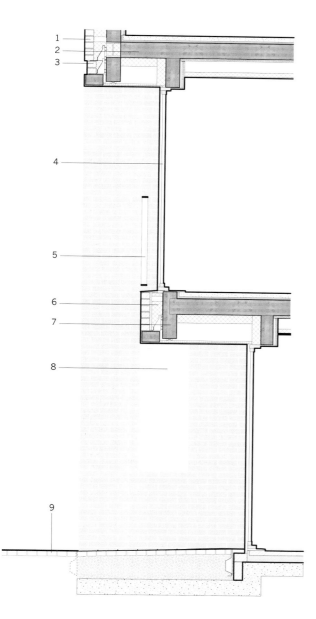

Detail section

1 Brickwork finish to external wall
2 CLT structural wall
3 Brickwork setback for shadow gap
4 High-performance double-glazing composite timber/
   aluminum door system
5 Flat steel galvanized and pre-coated balustrade
6 Thermal insulation
7 Main structure of cross-laminated timber
8 High-performance double-glazing composite timber/
   aluminum window system
9 Level access/brickwork

early detection. When members of the client group expressed their concerns about this approach, the design team organized a demonstration for residents. Fears were allayed when they saw how difficult it was to ignite a CLT panel, and how predictably it performed under fire conditions.

From the Borough's perspective, the construction of Bridport House met or exceeded all its expectations. The erection of the CLT panel structure was completed in just ten weeks, with an average of only one truck per day delivering CLT panels to the site. Panel installation was clean and quiet when compared to site-based construction in steel or concrete. With an installation crew of only five or six workers, additional traffic in the vicinity of the site was minimal.

CONCLUSION

While underscoring the many practical advantages of Tall Wood construction in the context of urban densification, this project also supports the related environmental arguments. To meet UK planning regulations, most large buildings are required to produce 10% of their energy demand from on-site renewable sources. In the case of Bridport House, however, the design team argued successfully that the CO_2 embodied in the structure, plus the CO_2 emissions saved by not building in concrete meant that the building would be carbon-positive for the first 27 years of operation.

STRANDPARKEN HUS B

Sundbyberg, Sweden [Wingårdh Arkitektkontor]

2012	**Year**
Folkhem	**Client**
Martinsons	**Structural Engineer**
Martinsons	**Engineered Wood Fabricator**
Folkhem Produktion AB	**Contractor**
Residential	**Program**

With its pitched roof and skin of western red cedar shingles, Stockholm's first Tall Wood project offers a new aesthetic for multi-storey CLT residential buildings.

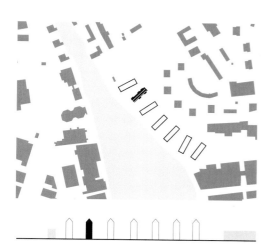

The site is located in Sundbyberg, a small and densely populated municipality in metropolitan Stockholm.

With its traditional domestic gable form and natural materials, Strandparken Hus B represents a departure from the flat roofs and hard finishes that are characteristic of many CLT apartment buildings.

With an area of only 8.8 square kilometres and more than 44,000 inhabitants, Sundbyberg is Sweden's smallest and most densely populated municipality. It lies within the Stockholm metropolitan area, to the north of the city centre. Sundbyberg is integrated into Stockholm's multi-modal transit system, but in other respects is quite self-contained. With numerous parks and forested areas as well as its own retail and commercial centre, Sundbyberg has become a highly desirable place to live.

CONCEPT

Strandparken is part of a broader initiative of brownfield redevelopment taking place across the metropolitan area of Stockholm. The site borders Lake Mälaren, and as such was recognized as having great potential for a more exclusive kind of residential development. To this end, the architects proposed a series of narrow-plan buildings, with generous apartments taking advantage of the views across the water. The architects also proposed that the buildings, including two eight-storey towers, be constructed of wood, setting a precedent in terms of scale for both the developer and the municipality.

The pitched roof and cedar shingle cladding of Strandparken Hus B represent a departure from the rectilinear geometry and hard exterior finishes typical of most other CLT apartment buildings completed to date. The form echoes that of many similar structures built during Sweden's post-World War II housing boom, while the large balconies and the use of natural materials speak to contemporary market aspirations.

CONSTRUCTION

For Folkhem, a developer with past experience only in small residential projects, the decision to embark on a prefabricated CLT building of this scale was a courageous one. The project team drew on the experience of Martinsons, the fabricator and installer of the CLT panels used on the precedent-setting Limnologen project in Växjö in 2009. To familiarize its own workers with some of the site procedures and finishing details that would be different on a project of this scale, Folkhem used two existing barracks buildings on the site

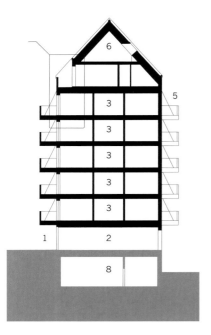

Section AA

1 Entrance
2 Lobby
3 Apartment
4 Bathroom
5 Balcony
6 Attic space
7 Stair and elevator core
8 Parking

During construction, workers and the site were protected by a tent. The prefabricated CLT wall panels were supplied complete with door and window openings, insulation and exterior and interior finishes. A crane lifted the prefabricated panels into place.

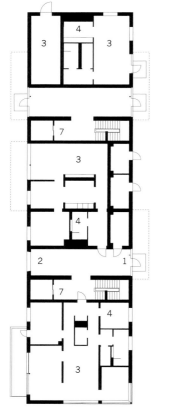

Ground floor plan

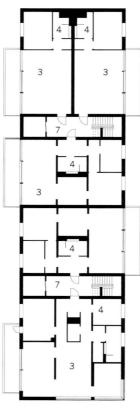

Typical floor plan

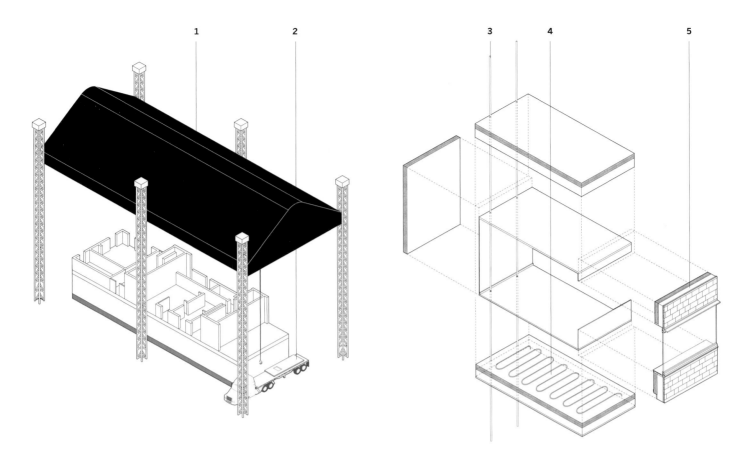

Diagram of construction sequence

1 During construction, the building was protected with a tent mounted on scaffolding that could be extended as work progressed. **2** The prefabricated wall and floor panels, complete with doors, windows and cedar shingle cladding, were delivered to site on flatbed trucks. **3** Panels were lifted into place by a bridge crane that spanned the length of the building. **4** The light structure was anchored by 23 steel tie rods, continuous from the roof to the concrete foundation. **5** The floor structure comprises a shallow raised wood floor that conceals a hydronic radiant heating system, 120mm thick CLT panels, acoustic insulation and an independently supported suspended ceiling.

for training purposes. This included test installations of the proposed western red cedar shingle cladding. The eight-storey Hus B building has a gross floor area of 4060 square metres, and includes 31 apartments ranging in size from 55 to 150 square metres. Construction is of the platform type, in which CLT interior and exterior walls support the CLT floor panels for the next storey, and these in turn create a platform for the following set of walls. In some locations, glulam beams are used to create longer spans over balcony openings or larger unobstructed interior spaces. Since starting CLT production in 2003, Martinsons has developed a standardized approach to component design for exterior walls, demising walls between suites, and interior partitions. At Strandparken, the exterior

wall panels are of a consistent 450mm thickness throughout the height of the building, comprising a 120mm thick CLT panel, three layers of 70mm thick insulation, sheathing paper, battens and cedar shingles. The interior faces of the panels are lined with 15mm gypsum wallboard. Panels are factory-cut and shipped to site with doors, windows and cladding installed as appropriate. On this project, the exterior wall panels were fabricated complete with the western red cedar shingle cladding. All panels are light enough to be off-loaded using only a truck-mounted crane. Erection took place beneath a tent, designed to protect both the workers and the wood from exposure to weather. As construction proceeded, this tent was raised using a self-stabilizing traveling structure. A

The interiors feature pine panels that were delivered to the site as prefabricated units.

The exterior of the building is finished in western red cedar shingles, a naturally durable material that will weather over time to a silver grey colour.

bridge crane (spanning between towers at either end of the building) permitted free movement of materials beneath the tent.

For the Strandparken Hus B project, the timber structure was erected on top of a semi-basement concrete parking garage, which not only protects the wood from exposure to surface water or physical damage, but also anchors the lightweight superstructure to the ground. Continuous steel tie rods extend from the concrete slab to the attic storey, resisting uplift due to wind. The lateral resistance for the structure is provided by a combination of CLT stair and elevator shafts, and the multiple CLT partitions that perform as shear walls.

Fire protection is provided by sprinklers in each unit and a fire-retardant treatment on the cedar shingles at ground floor level. Impact sound transmission through the floors is minimized with the installation of acoustic ceilings below the structural floors that are independently supported by a ledger attached to the walls. Heating is via a hydronic system concealed within a shallow raised floor. Thermal bridging through the wall assemblies is minimized by designing the balconies as separate structures suspended from the outside of the building.

CONCLUSION

With this first building being very much a prototype for the developer, it was estimated that the overall cost exceeded that of a conventional concrete building by approximately 12%. As the other phases are implemented, it is anticipated that manufacturing and assembly efficiencies will reduce the construction time and ultimately eliminate this cost premium.

The success of the Strandparken Hus B project confirms the acceptance of Tall Wood construction within a competitive and discerning residential market. It is also a breakthrough project for Sweden's largest metropolitan area, which, despite the lifting of the two-storey maximum height for wood buildings in the national building code in 1996, had been reluctant to permit taller wood structures.

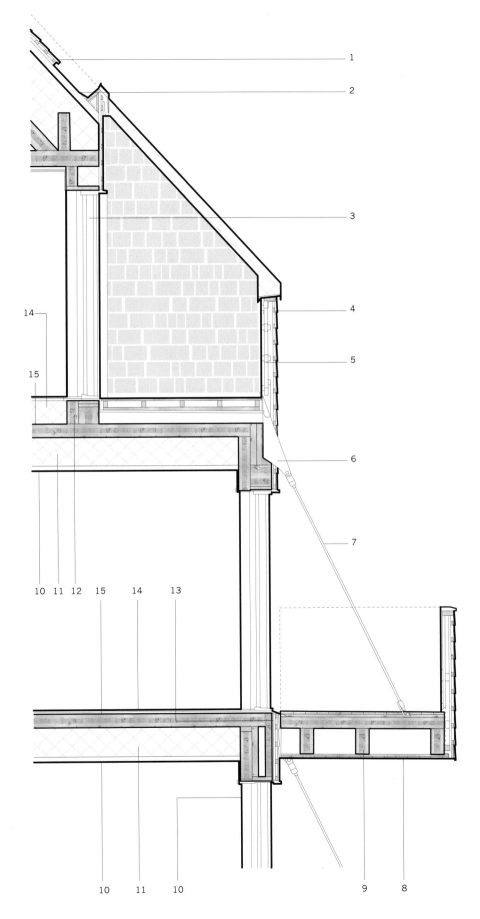

Detail section

1. 19mm roof shingles concealing EPDM roofing membrane
2. Titan zinc channel for water and snow
3. Exterior patio glazing (sliding door)
4. 19mm western red cedar shingles on battens
5. Plywood
6. Galvanized steel support bracket
7. Steel suspension rod
8. Weather-resistant thermowood 92mm × 21mm
9. Glulam beam 140mm × 270mm
10. Gypsum board 2mm × 13mm
11. Insulation 240mm
12. Glulam beam (over opening)
13. Thermal break assembly
14. 145mm deep raised wood floor to accommodate hydronic radiant heating
15. CLT floor panel bearing on CLT wall

VIA CENNI SOCIAL HOUSING

Milan, Italy [Rossiprodi Associati]

2013	**Year**
Polaris Real Estate SGR SpA	**Client**
Borlini & Zanini SA	**Structural Engineer**
Carron	**General Contractor**
MAK Holz	**Wood Consultant**
Stora Enso	**Engineered Wood Fabricator**
Service Legno	**Engineered Wood Installer**
Residential	**Program**

Located in Italy's most expensive city and in a highly seismic zone, the most important goals of this 124-unit residential project were affordability and safety.

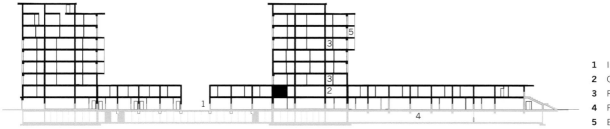

Section AA

1 Interior courtyard
2 Commercial space
3 Residence
4 Parking
5 Balcony

Via Cenni includes a large communal courtyard for the four CLT towers.

Europe's largest CLT residential complex is located in suburban Milan, where the compact blocks of the traditional city transition into the more open pattern of the modern metropolis. It is an area dotted with single-use developments, interspersed with farm fields and large parks. While there are many services to be found in the vicinity, the area lacks a defining character and social heart where residents can come together as a community. In addition, Milan is Italy's most expensive city and the provision of affordable housing is a pressing concern. Therefore, the goal for the Via Cenni project was to use a combination of innovative financing and state-of-the-art massive timber technology to deliver a high-quality, cost-competitive project that would offer its low- and middle-income residents a variety of rental and lease-to-own options.

CONCEPT

In response to the disparate physical context, the driving architectural ambition for the project was to create opportunities for social engagement, using a variety of building forms to acknowledge and support the demographic diversity of the residents. The primary generator of form is the dynamic flow of public and semi-public open space, which encourages integration between different services and functions and between the community and the district. Organized around this open space, the 30,000 square metre program, comprising 124 apartment units, common areas and ancillary commercial and retail spaces, is divided into four similar (though not identical) nine-storey towers, connected by several lower structures. These lower structures are inspired by the design of the traditional

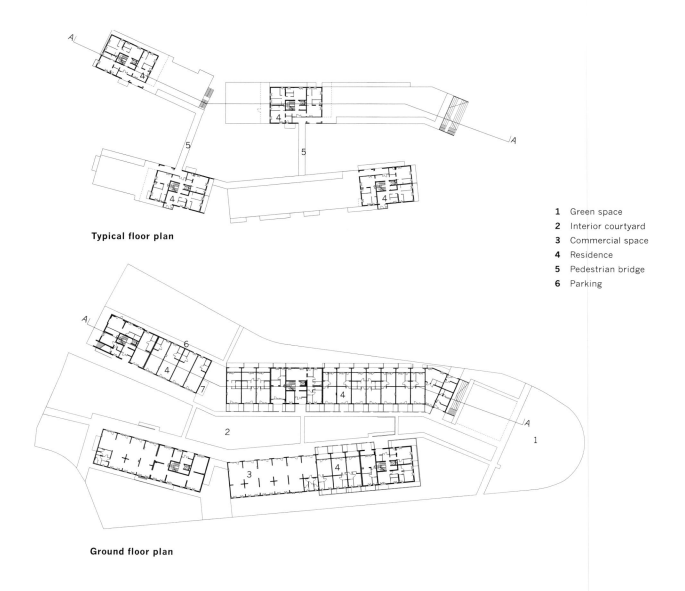

Typical floor plan

1 Green space
2 Interior courtyard
3 Commercial space
4 Residence
5 Pedestrian bridge
6 Parking

Ground floor plan

farmhouses of the region, in which long, linear buildings have a direct relationship with the adjacent open space. At the heart of the complex, a grand courtyard is animated by the retail and commercial activities dispersed around its perimeter.

CONSTRUCTION

In April 2009, an earthquake centred on the Italian town of L'Aquila resulted in the death of more than 300 people. Although almost 500 kilometres south of Milan, the reaction from regulators was to require all new buildings to conform to the country's most stringent seismic design criteria. In addition, while several CLT structures had been constructed for the winter Olympic Games in Turin in 2006 (and many other low-rise residential buildings since), Italian building regulations still limited the height of wood structures to three storeys for reasons of fire safety. As a result, the

design team was required to present its design proposals to the Ministry of Infrastructure and Transport for peer review and approval.

Although connected in plan, the four towers are structurally independent of the lower buildings that surround them. This was done to standardize the structural design and simplify the analysis of seismic performance. Sitting on a concrete basement structure, the towers measure 13.5 × 19.0 metres in plan and are constructed using load-bearing CLT wall and floor panels in a platform arrangement.

The five-ply CLT floor panels are stitched together to create continuous diaphragms of consistent thickness, either 200 or 230mm in depth. The interior walls are regularly spaced, and where possible, superimposed one on top of another through all nine floors of the building. This creates three continuous shear walls in one direction and four in the other direction. The

Holes are drilled for the bolt and plate connections used on the lowest three floors.

The CLT elevator shaft is part of the lateral system for each building.

The large scale of the site created logistical challenges.

A crane was used to lift and manoeuvre CLT panels into position.

exterior walls are designed with a highly regular pattern of punched window openings. A few larger openings are spanned by glulam lintels, but this does not alter the overall cellular character of the system, which is designed to distribute and dissipate seismic and other forces evenly throughout the structure. The five-ply CLT wall panels reduce in thickness (and hence stiffness) from 200mm on the lowest floor to 120mm on the top floor. Stair and elevator cores are also constructed of CLT. Overall, the CLT structure is approximately one sixth the weight of a concrete equivalent, which greatly reduces the magnitude of any seismic forces acting upon it.

Two types of connection were developed to join the CLT wall and floor panels. The first type is used on the first three floors, and also to anchor the CLT wall panels on the ground floor to the concrete basement structure. It consists of steel T-plates located at the top and bottom of the wall panels and fastened to them using 7mm dowels. The flanges of the T-plates are connected together by 16mm bolts passing through the floor panels.

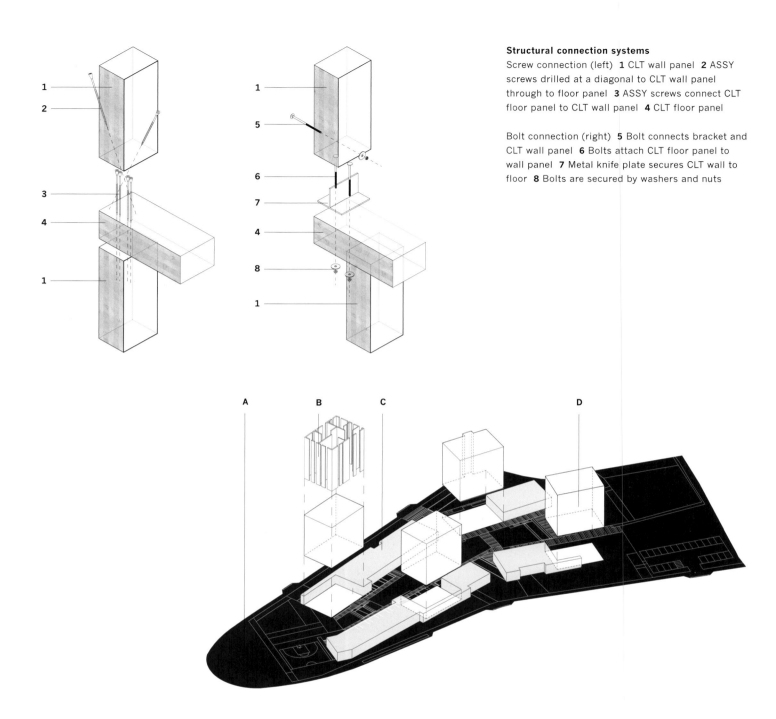

Structural connection systems

Screw connection (left) **1** CLT wall panel **2** ASSY screws drilled at a diagonal to CLT wall panel through to floor panel **3** ASSY screws connect CLT floor panel to CLT wall panel **4** CLT floor panel

Bolt connection (right) **5** Bolt connects bracket and CLT wall panel **6** Bolts attach CLT floor panel to wall panel **7** Metal knife plate secures CLT wall to floor **8** Bolts are secured by washers and nuts

Volumetric organization

A Outdoor sports courts, walkways, communal areas and parking surround the four main buildings. **B** Shear walls are connected to form a continuous network of structural support. **C** A lower podium building with common areas links the four towers. **D** The towers accommodate affordable housing.

The second type is used on the upper floors of the tower and relies solely on self-tapping screws. Pairs of screws are inserted at an angle of 45° in opposing directions from either side of the panel. Closely spaced, these screws essentially stitch the CLT panels together, creating a continuous connection with high stiffness that transfers loads efficiently and evenly from one panel to another. The site installation of this connection is very straightforward, and permits the correction of minor inconsistencies in alignment of the panels. The result is a unified three-dimensional structural

A large communal square provides outdoor space for the residents.

Sports courts and seating are built into the landscape.

system in which seismic forces can be effectively distributed and dissipated throughout the building. Exposed interior CLT surfaces are protected from fire by a layer of drywall mounted on battens. The void created between the drywall and the wood is used to run conduit, sprinkler pipes and other services. The exterior cladding is cement stucco. The entire structure was completed in 16 months, approximately 50% faster than a conventional concrete frame equivalent. The cost of the wood structure was calculated to be 19% cheaper than concrete.

CONCLUSION

This project has proven to be very popular with its residents who, in addition to appreciating the sense of community it inspires, find it quiet and comfortable in all seasons, and very inexpensive to heat and cool. With its simple, economical and highly replicable construction details, Via Cenni has demonstrated the viability of Tall Wood construction in seismic zones, and has prompted code changes that will further encourage the use of this technology.

WOODCUBE

Hamburg, Germany [Architekturagentur Stuttgart]

2013	**Year**
DeepGreen Development	**Client**
Isenmann Ingenieure	**Structural Engineer**
Thoma Holz 100 GmbH	**Engineered Wood Fabricator**
Residential	**Program**

This project explores the many environmentally beneficial attributes of wood, offering a new vision for urban living that goes beyond energy efficiency to embrace life cycle impacts and occupant health.

The CLT panels cantilever 2.5 metres beyond the building to create generous balconies.

From 2006 to 2013, the city of Hamburg was host to the International Building Exhibition (IBA), a unique initiative that devised and implemented 70 innovative planning and building projects, exploring environmentally responsible and socially balanced forms of urban redevelopment. These projects, conceived in part around ideas of decentralized renewable energy strategies and the efficient use of local resources, now form the nucleus of urban renewal efforts on the mostly industrial island of Wilhelmsburg in the River Elbe. The IBA's legacy includes the Woodcube, a 1,370 square metre, five-storey apartment building constructed almost entirely from wood. The in-depth research that underpins the innovative design has confirmed the versatility of wood, its potential contribution to sustainable development and its effectiveness in addressing many aspects of building performance.

CONCEPT

From an urban design perspective, the Woodcube was conceived as a prototype for a systematized yet flexible approach to the design and construction of multi-family residential buildings. At the same time, the design team wanted to broaden the discussion of sustainability from one focused largely on the operating energy of buildings, to one that embraces carbon-neutral construction and a healthy indoor environment.

CONSTRUCTION

Low-energy buildings, such as those constructed to the Passive House standard, typically rely on a tightly sealed and highly insulated envelope to control heat gain and loss. Often the materials used for vapour checks and insulation are manufactured using harmful chemicals that can release toxins into the air long

The building is part of the Wilhelmsburg Central Integrated Energy Network, which provides heat from renewable sources.

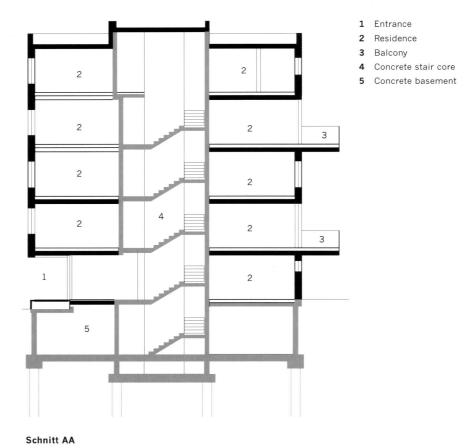

1	Entrance
2	Residence
3	Balcony
4	Concrete stair core
5	Concrete basement

Schnitt AA

The CLT panels are left exposed and unfinished on the interior of the building. Artificial lighting is provided by low-energy LED fixtures.

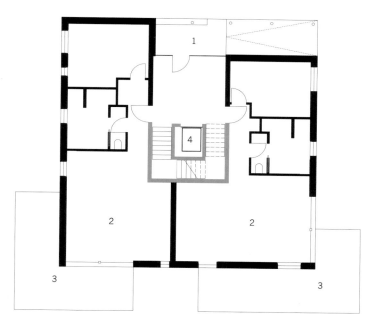

Ground floor plan

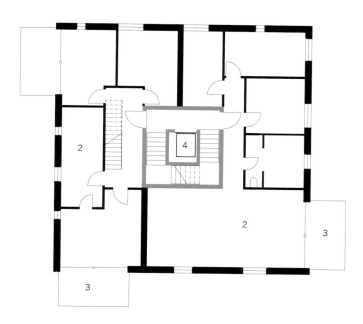

Typical floor plan

Wall and floor assembly

The Woodcube uses no glue or adhesives, instead the dry fit CLT wall and floor panels are connected with high-strength ASSY screws to form the connection points. **1** ASSY screws inserted at a diagonal into both roof and wall CLT **2** CLT roof panel with edge grooves for form fitting of assemblies **3** CLT dry fit wall panel **4** ASSY screws connect the walls, the ends of the walls have grooves to connect the corners.

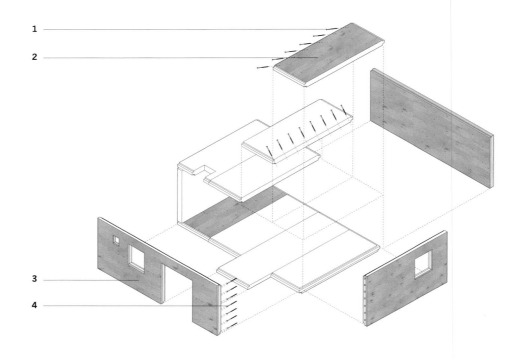

The Woodcube was built using prefabricated wall and floor/ceiling panels. During construction and until the roof was in place, the assemblies were kept dry using tarps and scaffolding.

after installation. Similarly, some materials used to encapsulate or sheathe a structure to achieve the fire resistance required in a multi-storey building also emit harmful vapours or give off dust.

Furthermore, most low-energy building standards focus exclusively on the reduction of operating energy, and do not concern themselves with the source of that energy. Nor do these standards consider the embodied energy present in the materials used to construct the building, or the carbon footprint, life cycle implications or other environmental impacts of those materials. Hence the design team chose to start with locally sourced, sustainably managed wood, a 'smart'[1] multi-functional material that in principle met all these criteria; and, through research and testing, develop solu-

tions that would meet their own performance requirements, as well as those of the applicable building codes.

The Woodcube is a 15.10 metre square in plan, with exterior load-bearing walls and a central concrete stair and elevator core that rises from a concrete basement structure. There are no intermediate supports and apartments are subdivided with non-load-bearing wood frame partitions to facilitate future reconfiguration. Flexibility is further enhanced by clustering service risers against the exterior walls. The Woodcube comprises eight apartments of different types, including both single level and maisonette units.

The walls, floors and roof are made from prefabricated solid wood panels that are cross-laminated in

Connection to central core

A central concrete core houses the stairs and resists lateral loads on the structure.

1 Roof panels connect to one another **2** Concrete core with stairs **3** Metal C-brackets connect the CLT panels to the concrete core. **4** Roof panels are cut to fit around the concrete core. **5** After installation the floor receives insulating boards, sound insulation and a wooden floor system.

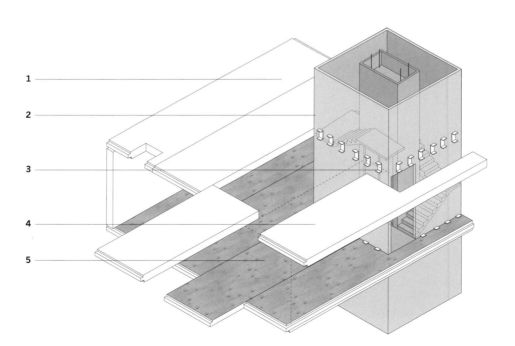

The floor structure spans from the service core to the exterior wall creating uninterrupted interior space.

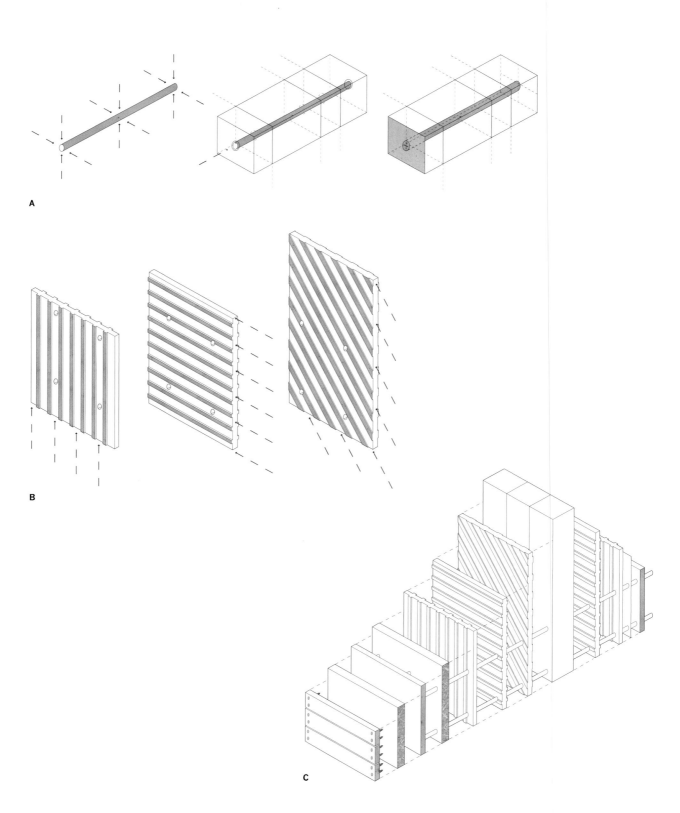

Glueless cross-laminated timber

A The CLT panels employ no adhesives. Instead the wall was designed with beech wood dowels inserted through the layers of the wall. The dowel is kiln-dried below the moisture content of the other components and expands to create a tight fit as it reaches its equilibrium moisture content. **B** The CLT panels in the exterior walls are milled with a pattern of shallow grooves in diagonal, horizontal and vertical directions. They trap air and increase the thermal insulation value of the walls. **C** The pre-made wall panels are composed of 12 layers of wood and mineral wool. These layers are dry fit together and act as the main structure while providing a high degree of thermal resistance.

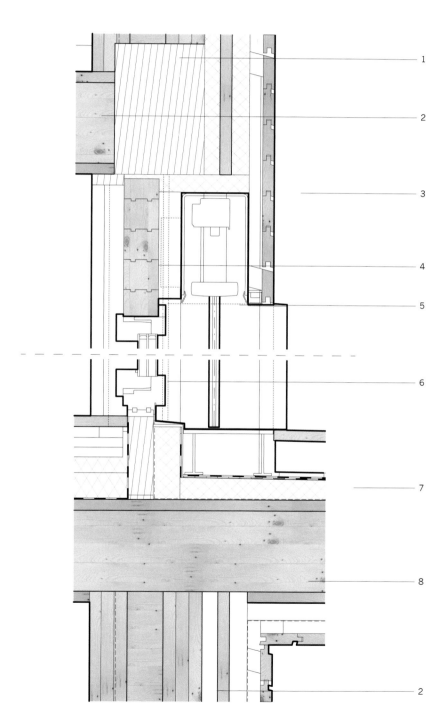

Detail section

1 Wood beam
2 CLT wall assembly
3 Internal wall cladding
4 Exterior wall cladding
5 Sliding door system
6 Triple pane glazing
7 Wooden flooring
8 CLT floor assembly

The exterior is clad in unfinished, horizontal larch siding; note the exhaust vents and metal lines indicating the fire compartments.

layers of horizontal, vertical and diagonal boards. The layers are mechanically fastened using beech dowels inserted into holes drilled perpendicular to the face of the panels on a 240mm x 300mm grid. The bond between layers is achieved by kiln drying the dowels, inserting them into tight-fit holes, then allowing them to expand until they reach their equilibrium moisture content. This creates a friction fit, and a panel with comparable strength to conventional CLT, without the need for adhesives. The dry, single-material construction makes it possible for these panels to be dismantled and individual components reclaimed simply by 'reverse programming' the same CNC machines used to fabricate them.

The wall panels are 320mm thick, comprising (from inside to outside) a 251mm thick panel of dowelled and cross-laminated fir boards (within which is an 80mm solid wood core), a 44mm layer of softwood fibreboard insulation and a 29mm layer of fir boards. Structural loads are carried by the solid wood cores, which line up vertically from floor to floor. The remainder of the 250mm wood thickness serves as a sacrificial layer for fire resistance.

The CLT floor panels span 6 metres between the exterior walls and the central service core. Only where the panels extend beyond the building to form balconies is a steel and wood composite beam required to increase panel stiffness. These beams are the same depth as the panels themselves, maintaining a flush ceiling surface to permit flexibility in the placement of interior walls.

The exterior finish for the Woodcube is untreated larch panels, detailed to create mini compartments (500mm in height) behind the cladding, rather than a continuous rainscreen cavity. This is to prevent the spread of flames upwards in the event of fire. A cellulose-based sealing foil within the wall assembly prevents smoke infiltration into the building, and also acts as a air barrier. The assembly was tested for compliance with local fire codes, and is the first non-encapsulated system to meet the requirements of Germany's Category 4 (two-hour fire resistance) classification without the need for sprinklers or a standpipe.

The wall assembly has a thermal transmittance of 0.19W/m²/°C (R53 equivalent). Baseline thermal performance was enhanced by milling grooves into the individual board layers, providing macroscopic non-circulating air cushions that further reduce the thermal conductivity of the walls. With the roof assembly having a thermal transmittance of 0.105W/m²/°C (R95 equivalent), the Woodcube achieves an annual operating energy consumption of 18KWh/m² – very close to Passive House standard. This energy is supplied from renewable sources including a rooftop photovoltaic array. The vapour-open wall assembly means that the risk of condensation and mould growth is virtually eliminated, and the panels carry a 50-year manufacturer's warranty in this regard. The carbon stored in the wood panels more than offsets the carbon footprint of the concrete and steel components, making the Woodcube carbon-neutral or even carbon-positive over its anticipated 50-year service life.

CONCLUSION

The Woodcube capitalizes on the multiple environmental attributes of wood, including its application as a bio-fuel, its low embodied energy, its ability to sequester and store carbon, its thermal characteristics, its performance in fire and its contribution to healthy indoor environments. While the building is not cost-competitive with current market equivalents, it establishes important precedents that are potentially transformative. It also repositions wood as an inherently 'smart' material that plays an active role in many aspects of building physics.

REFERENCES

1   'Smart Materials', i.e. materials that change with time to mitigate the environmental forces acting on a building, was one of the themes of IBA 2013.

PUUKUOKKA HOUSING BLOCK

Jyväskylä, Finland [OOPEAA]

2015	**Year**
Lakea and City of Jyväskylä	**Client**
Stora Enso	**Structural Engineer**
Stora Enso	**Engineered Wood Fabricator**
Keski-Suomen Rakennuslinja	**Contractor**
Residential	**Program**

Exploiting the potential of volumetric prefabrication, this project embodies a radical new approach to the design and delivery of Tall Wood buildings.

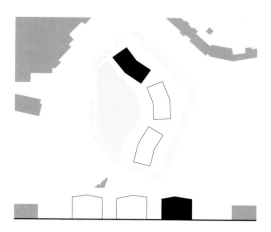

Site plan and elevation

One façade of building is stained black while the other is a natural larch finish.

Situated on the north shore of Lake Päijänne amid the hills and forests of central Finland, Jyväskylä is a fast-growing city of about 140,000 inhabitants. It has long been known for the quality of its higher education institutions, which underpin an economy now based on healthcare services, IT and renewable energy technology. Architecturally, the city is best known for its unrivalled collection of works by the great Finnish Modernist Alvar Aalto.

This culture of innovation makes Jyväskylä an appropriate setting for the realization of Finland's first eight-storey CLT apartment building. Puukuokka Housing Block capitalizes on recent changes to the country's building codes, and also implements new approaches to project delivery that emerged from a critical self-examination by Finland's wood products and construction industries. Previously fragmented and focused on individual products, industry stakeholders realized they could not capitalize on the opportunities presented by new materials such as CLT, or new technologies such as digital fabrication, without a shared vision.

Restrictive building codes, a shortage of skilled carpenters, and a development industry used to design/build project delivery, meant that the introduction of locally produced CLT to the market could not by itself be a catalyst for change. Rather, it was necessary for industry stakeholders to integrate the material into a new and holistic approach to building that would reposition wood as an appropriate and desirable material for larger projects.

CONCEPT

Completed in 2015, the Puukuokka Housing Block is the first phase in a proposed three-building complex designed by architects OOPEAA in collaboration with developer Lakea and the Jyväskylä City Planning Department. When completed, the complex will comprise 150 apartments with a net floor area of approximately 10,000 square metres.

The Puukuokka project explores the potential of modular prefabricated CLT construction to meet the municipality's goal of providing high-quality, environmentally responsible and affordable housing for its

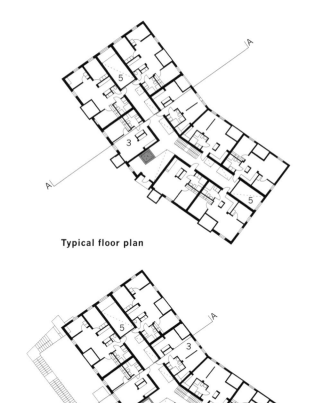

Typical floor plan

Ground floor plan

1 Landscaped entrance
2 Entrance and atrium
3 Apartment
4 Outdoor patio space
5 Atrium
6 Parking
7 Balcony

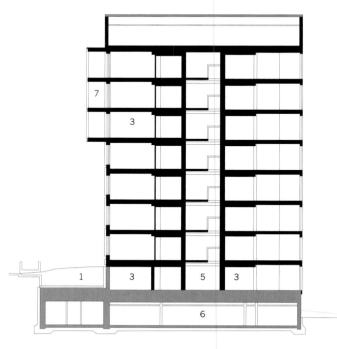

Section AA

citizens. Phase 1 includes apartments that range in size from 54 square metres for one-bedroom units to 76 square metres for three-bedroom units.

With a strong social and environmental mandate, durable, cost-effective, low-carbon construction was also seen as a prerequisite for the introduction of an innovative lease-to-own financing strategy. This concept supports social sustainability by promoting stable communities. A 7% down payment on the purchase price of an apartment enables a purchaser to secure a state-guaranteed loan and, after a rental period of 20 years, assume freehold ownership of the unit.

CONSTRUCTION

The building follows the contours of the site in order to minimize disturbance to the underlying bedrock and existing vegetation. Above the cast-in-place concrete basement parking level, the building consists of volumetric prefabricated apartment modules made up from spruce CLT panels. OOPEAA worked closely with

CLT manufacturer Stora Enso to develop a system of load-bearing modules that could capitalize on the benefits of factory production without compromising the architectural ambitions of the project. The stacked modules are capable of carrying the required vertical loads up to the eight-storey maximum height permitted by code.

In northern climates in particular, with their long and harsh winters, prefabrication offers many advantages both in terms of quality and cost control. For Puukuokka, each apartment consists of two prefabricated modules – one 'wet' and one 'dry'. The dry module includes the living room, the balcony and the bedroom, while the wet module houses the bathroom, the kitchen and the foyer area. To ensure the most efficient use of material, OOPEAA carefully controlled module dimensions to minimize waste.

Completed modules, including floor and wall finishes, kitchen and bathroom fixtures, were transported to the site on a just-in-time basis, to be stacked like Lego

The interior corridors terminate in day-lit atria that rise through all eight storeys of the building.

The interior atrium provides generous amounts of light and fresh air to the internal corridor of Puukuokka.

A Balcony (cold)
B Apartment (warm)
C Balcony (semi-warm)
D Apartment (warm)
1 CLT structural panel
2 Roof of balcony

3 Air gap
4 Concrete screed layer and integrated underfloor heating
5 Insulation 100mm
6 Sliding glass door system
7 Insulation 50mm

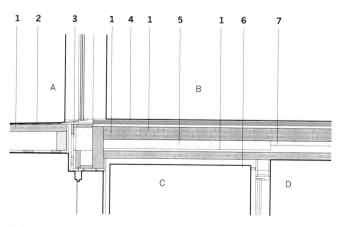

Balcony section

bricks on either side of a central void that would become the circulation spine. Wall thicknesses decrease from the bottom to the top of the building, reflecting the lighter loads carried by the upper storeys.

The roof was prefabricated on site in sections. The size of the site made it possible to fabricate a temporary roof structure that could be lifted from the ground and placed on top of each completed storey of modules as construction progressed. Prior to the arrival of the next set of modules, the roof would be removed and placed back on the ground. This approach to weather protection was justifiable because of the high value and vulnerability of the fully finished prefabricated modules.

All central services, including electricity and piping for heat and water, are installed in vertical risers integrated into the hallway walls. This enables apartment modules to be easily 'plugged in', and facilitates access for ongoing maintenance and repairs. The corridors are formed by CLT 'bridge' panels that span

Housing block under construction. Modular units are delivered by truck and lifted into place by crane.

Construction sequences

1 The façade is applied to the modular system once the structure is complete. **2** 'Dry' pre-made modules come to the site complete with interior fittings. **3** 'Wet' modules come to the site with toilet and sink installed. **4** Vertical service ducts are integrated between the prefabricated modules and the site-built interior hallway. **5** Railing system **6** Built on site, the atria at either end of the building extend the full height of the building and admit abundant natural light and air to both sides of the units. **7** CLT stairs connect the floors. **8** Once assembled, the frame system together with the wall and floor panels becomes structurally rigid. **9** The walls of the interior hallways provide bracing against shear and lateral movements.

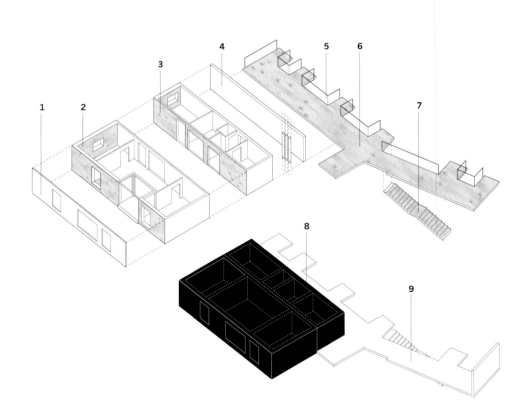

On the street façade the spruce cladding is painted black, and the majority of the balconies are recessed.

between the opposing stacks of modules. A sense of openness is apparent in these shared spaces, which are generously planned, with ample daylight and views to the surrounding landscape. The corridors terminate in atria that extend the full height of the building. Punched windows admit natural light, and automated ventilation louvres in the roof prevent smoke build-up in the event of a fire. The building is sprinklered throughout and exposed wood surfaces are finished with a flame-retardant coating.

The apartment modules have a factory-installed concrete topping with in-floor electric radiant heating and a parquet finish. The CLT ceilings are left exposed, an alternative solution that required the involvement of a fire protection engineer. The walls are finished in gypsum wallboard in conformance with Finnish fire regulations, but also provide a visual complement to the horizontal wood surfaces.

Between the ceiling of one unit and the floor of the unit above, mineral fibre insulation is used to reduce noise transmission. The fact that ceiling and floor are independent systems further reduces the transmission of impact noise. Where occupied spaces have recessed balconies above or below, the thickness is increased from 50mm to 100mm to provide the required level of thermal insulation.

Externally, the building exhibits a dual character, with one long elevation being its public face, the other its private face. On the courtyard side, the prefabricated larch panels are left unfinished and will weather to a silver grey. This façade is animated with protruding balconies. On the street façade, the spruce cladding has been finished with a dark paint and the majority of balconies are recessed and enclosed with sliding glass doors. Exterior walls have a 180mm layer of mineral wool insulation between the structural CLT panel and the wood cladding.

CONCLUSION

Puukuokka is an excellent example of productive collaboration between architects, engineers and industry. It can be seen as a prototype for a radical new approach to the design and delivery of mid- and high-rise apartment buildings, one that responds to the opportunities and constraints of the local construction industry. It offers the promise of higher quality and more environmentally responsible construction, delivered at a competitive price.

FRAME SYSTEMS

Frame systems, in which vertical loads are carried by an interconnected system of beams and columns, lend themselves naturally to building programs that require larger and more flexible interior spaces, typically commercial, institutional and assembly occupancies. Frame systems provide the opportunity for larger areas of glazing and therefore a different architectural expression than that associated with residential buildings. They also require additional measures, such as cross bracing or shear walls, to address issues of lateral stability.

Different approaches to the design of frame systems are illustrated in the following portfolio of projects:

– The Earth Sciences Building combines a traditional post-and-beam frame with contemporary approaches to connection design and wood/concrete composite construction.
– The Tamedia Head Office exploits the potential of digital fabrication to create a structure inspired by traditional Japanese joinery techniques.
– The Bullitt Center has a glulam post-and-beam structure and nail-laminated floor panel construction that closely resembles that of late 19th and early 20th century commercial buildings.
– At the Wood Innovation and Design Centre lateral stability for the glulam post-and-beam frame is provided by the CLT elevator shaft and stair cores.

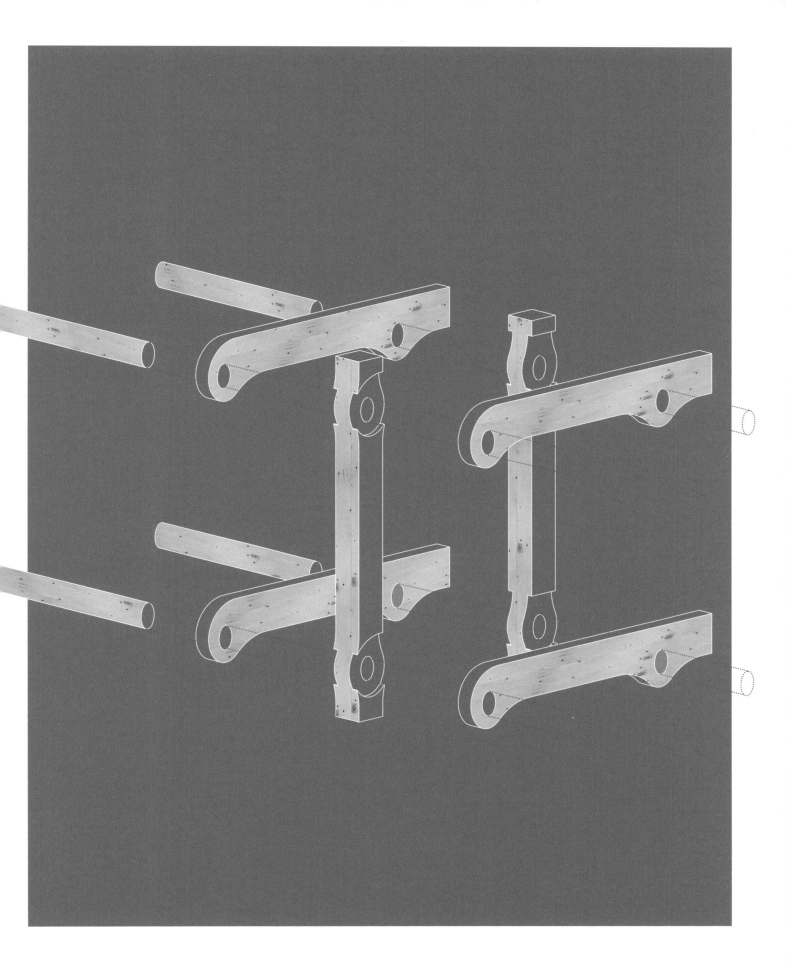

EARTH SCIENCES BUILDING

Vancouver, Canada [Perkins + Will]

2012	**Year**
University of British Columbia	**Client**
Equilibrium Consulting	**Structural Engineer**
Structurlam	**Engineered Wood Fabricator**
Bird Construction	**Construction Manager**
Education	**Program**

In response to its progressive academic program, this building explores the potential of new massive wood technology to meet the client's ambitious sustainability goals.

Glulam columns are featured in many parts of the building.

Located on the main campus of the University of British Columbia (UBC), the five-storey, 15,800 square metre Earth Sciences Building (ESB) was completed in August 2012. It consolidates teaching, laboratory and administrative spaces for several related departments previously dispersed around the campus.

The chosen site is in a prominent position, across the central thoroughfare of Main Mall from the existing Beatty Biodiversity Museum. As such the project offered the opportunity to complete a 'gateway' to a new science and engineering precinct. With this role in mind, the enhancement of the public realm and connectivity with the rest of the campus became important drivers of the design.

CONCEPT

These urban design ambitions informed an architectural approach based on external transparency, and an internal arrangement that would encourage the informal use of the building by others on campus. To this end, the design sought to provide not only state-of-the-art-formal academic space, but also flexible informal learning spaces conducive to collaboration and future adaptation.

The strategic location of the project, together with its progressive research program, supported the idea of a high-profile, technologically advanced building that could further the University's sustainability goals. With the emergence of modern massive timber construction in Europe, and the recent arrival of the technology in North America, UBC (which had two smaller mass timber projects already commissioned at the time) was open to exploring its potential further on the Earth Sciences Building.

CONSTRUCTION

The form of the building was driven by site constraints and opportunities, programmatic needs and the desire to maximize the use of passive environmental design strategies. The L-shaped plan comprises two wings, separated by a five-storey atrium upon which the external and internal circulation routes converge. A sculptural wood stair rises through the space, its unique cantilevered design made possible by the superior strength and increased stiffness of engineered wood products and advanced connection systems.

The higher-hazard occupancies (with their heavy equipment and complex servicing requirements) are located in the south wing, which has a concrete frame structure. Here, the majority of the program comprises laboratories and their related classroom and support spaces. The lower-hazard occupancies were accommodated in the north wing, which has a glulam post-and-beam frame structure with wood/concrete composite floors. Here the program comprises offices and three lecture theatres.

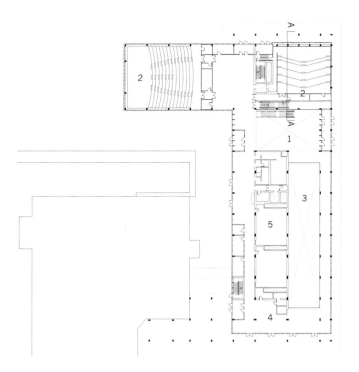

Ground floor plan

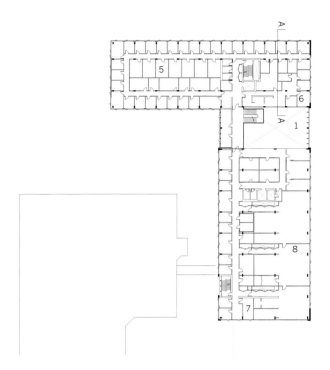

Typical floor plan

1 Atrium
2 Lecture theatre
3 High-head laboratories
4 Cafe
5 Classroom
6 Computer labs
7 Shared space
8 Labs

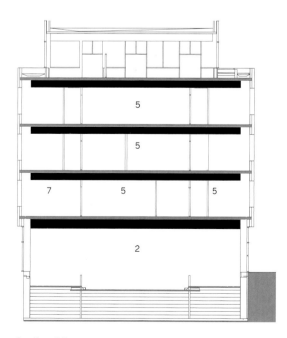

Section AA

The main public areas of the project, including the atrium, cafe, museum and informal learning spaces, are located on the ground floor, which is fully glazed to provide visual as well as physical connection to the surrounding campus. The 6.4 metre square structural grid was chosen to match that of the Beatty Biodiversity Museum opposite, as was the height of the horizontal canopy that wraps the east and south sides of the building. The canopy extends over the forecourt to engage the adjacent Fairview Commons, one of UBC's most important public open spaces. The Earth Sciences Building was one of the first projects in North America to incorporate advanced prefabrication methods, wood/concrete composite components and proprietary connection systems into a precisely engineered and detailed version of traditional heavy timber post-and-beam construction.

The north wing employs a glulam post-and-beam frame structure, a modified version of the balloon frame system. The glulam columns extend the full height of the building, and beams are connected into the face of the columns using proprietary Sherpa connectors. These steel connectors consist of two parts that are attached to the beam and column in the factory. Brought together on site, they form a contemporary steel version of the traditional wooden dovetail connection. The final appearance is very neat, with the

HBV mesh being installed in pre-cut grooves in LSL floor panels before the concrete topping is poured.

A modified HBV system is used to connect the treads and risers of the cantilevered stair.

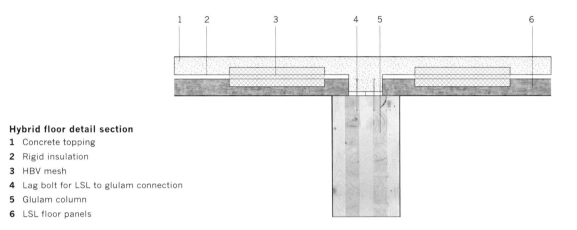

Hybrid floor detail section
1 Concrete topping
2 Rigid insulation
3 HBV mesh
4 Lag bolt for LSL to glulam connection
5 Glulam column
6 LSL floor panels

connectors concealed and protected from fire by the wood elements. End grain-to-end grain bearing columns were employed to minimize shrinkage.

Another innovative component of the project is the system of storey-height glulam chevron braces, which are left exposed on the interior of the building and are visible through the glazing of the south elevation. Together with a concrete stair shaft and the floor and roof diaphragms, they form the lateral system for the building. The braces themselves are rigid because of their triangular configuration, so that the dissipation of seismic forces takes place through the deformation of the multiple steel knife plate connectors.

Composite laminated strand lumber and concrete floors connected by the proprietary HBV system imported from Germany form the floor system. The construction of this floor system began with the installation of LSL panels spanning the 6.4 metres between beams. Once this structural subfloor was in place, the

installation of the HBV system required lengths of steel mesh to be inserted and epoxy-glued into kerfs cut into the LSL panels. A grid of rebar was then laid on 'chairs' and the concrete slab was poured to create a floor system with composite action. In addition to increased strength, the weight of the concrete reduces vibration and improves acoustic performance.

This was the first time that the HBV system had been used with LSL (chosen because the availability of CLT was uncertain at the time). Full-scale testing was carried out by FP Innovations, a Canadian forest products research organization, to confirm that performance of the floor would meet the design criteria.

The glulam frame for the entire building was erected and the LSL floors and roof were installed before pouring of the concrete slabs began. Concrete work started at the top of the building, providing a measure of weather protection for the lower levels as work progressed.

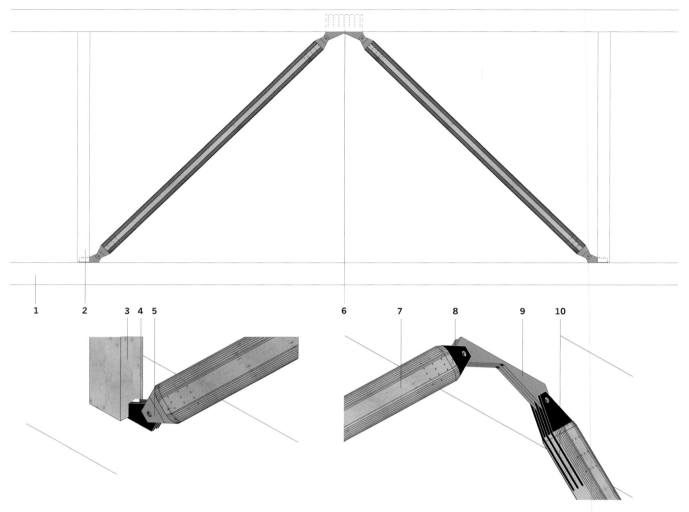

Chevron bracing system

1 The chevron support system sits on LSL floors. **2** Glulam columns hold floors and provide lateral support.
3 Glulam columns form end braces for chevrons, steel brackets are embedded within them. **4** A two-part steel
bracket distributes the forces from the bracing. **5** The lower pin bracket allows movement within the system.
6 The upper bracket is fitted to the glulam beam and forms a connection point between two diagonal braces.
7 Diagonal braces are tapered to a rounded square profile at the end. **8** The steel pin joint is fitted into the diagonal
bracing. **9** Metal bracing is two-pronged to provide support and connection areas. **10** Knife plates extend down into
the diagonal bracing, a gap at the bottom of the knife plates allows for movement.

Detail of glulam beam and column during
construction, forming a hidden connection.

Detail of chevron bracing system during construction. Metal knife plates extend into the
glulam beams to provide an angled connection.

A CLT canopy stretches from the exterior to the interior and provides shade.

The cantilevered stairs are featured prominently in the five-storey atrium.

As the height of the Earth Sciences Building exceeded that permitted by code for heavy timber construction for an institutional occupancy, an 'alternative solution' was required to demonstrate that the wood structure provided a level of fire safety equivalent to that of a non-combustible building.

The alternative solution included the following special measures: the separation of the program into high and low-hazard areas (with the high-hazard laboratories accommodated in the concrete south wing); the use of concealed connections for the timber structure, with steel components protected by wood; the underside of the LSL floor slabs being protected by suspended ceilings with a low flame spread rating; the installation of a sprinkler system; and the atrium stair not being used as a designated fire escape route.

The building is wrapped on two sides by an exterior canopy. Because the canopy was not a critical component in the overall project schedule, it was possible to construct it using prefabricated CLT panels fastened to the underside of glulam beams using lag screws. This results in a continuous flat soffit that creates a seamless connection between inside and outside space.

CONCLUSION

The Earth Sciences Building represents a pivotal moment in the evolution of massive timber construction in North America (mostly called 'mass timber' there). After the successful completion of several smaller-scale, mostly residential CLT buildings, it has demonstrated that contemporary massive timber technology can be successfully applied at a larger scale and to high-performance buildings of different occupancies.

TAMEDIA HEAD OFFICE

Zurich, Switzerland [Shigeru Ban Architects]

2013	**Year**
Tamedia AG	**Client**
Creation Holz GmbH	**Structural Engineer**
Blumer-Lehmann AG	**Engineered Wood Fabricator**
HRS Real Estate AG	**Contractor**
Office	**Program**

Inspired by traditional Japanese joinery, the intricate all-wood post-and-beam structure of this building was made possible by the precision of computerized fabrication.

The structural rhythm and mansard roof form of the building responds to the historic context of the site. The new building extends over the adjacent building, creating meeting and office spaces.

Located in the centre of Zurich, this project provides office accommodation for 500 employees of the Swiss media group Tamedia, consolidating its operations into a single urban campus. The new building replaces an existing structure, occupying the original footprint, but extending its two uppermost storeys over an adjacent structure to create a continuous street frontage of almost 50 metres facing the Sihl canal. The main axis of the building extends to the junction of Werdstrasse and Stauffacherquai, creating a new main entry for the entire Tamedia complex. The most striking feature of the building is its exposed wood structure, visible not only on the interior, but through the fully glazed double façade.

CONCEPT

As a creative company, Tamedia wanted to provide its employees with a relaxing yet inspiring work environment that would support informal interaction and collaboration. The choice of an exposed timber structure wrapped in an envelope of glass supported these ambitions, and the use of connection details inspired by traditional Japanese joinery techniques gives the interior the atmosphere of a domestic living room. The low embodied energy and the sequestered carbon of the 2000 cubic metres of spruce glulam incorporated in the wood structure, also contributes to Tamedia's corporate sustainability goals. The building has a low construction carbon footprint and, with its energy-efficient high-performance envelope and geo-exchange heating and cooling system, is carbon-neutral in its operations.

Accommodating the required program for a new and contemporary building within strict urban design guidelines, and constructing it on a restricted site adjacent to other fully operational buildings, presented both architectural and logistical challenges. The choice of a mansard roof form, and its extension over the adjacent building, maximized the program area within the permitted building height, while the choice of a prefabricated wood structure reduced the construction time and minimized noise and other forms of disruption to the occupants of surrounding buildings.

Site plan

Section AA

CONSTRUCTION

The desire for a fully glazed envelope and an exposed structure in which even the connections were to be of wood, presented challenges for the thermal and structural performance of the building. These issues have been addressed with an integrated approach that involves both programmatic and technical innovation. The entire east façade of the building has been designed as a full-height double-envelope system, with the intermediate space between the outer and inner layers of the glass curtain wall containing circulation stairs and lounge areas that overlook the city. The outer glass wall is operable, enabling the enclosed seating areas to become exterior terraces when the weather permits. Thus, in addition to forming part of the overall passive ventilation and energy strategies for the building, these areas, which are conditioned using extraction air from the adjacent offices, reinforce the

unique connection between the interior spaces of the building and its surrounding context. Special attention was given to the detailing of penetrations through the glass in order to achieve the low energy transmission levels required to conform to Zurich's strict energy performance requirements.

The main body of the building is 38.15 metres in length and 11 metres in width. It is spanned by eight structural frames set at 5.45 metres centres. Each frame consists of four equally spaced columns that extend the full 21 metre height of the building; a pair of transverse beams for each of the floors; and a series of longitudinal tie beams of oval cross section that pass through the beam pairs at each column position. Because of their oval shape, these tie beams cannot rotate, enabling them to absorb the lateral forces to which the building may be subjected, yet preventing the structural frame from deflecting.

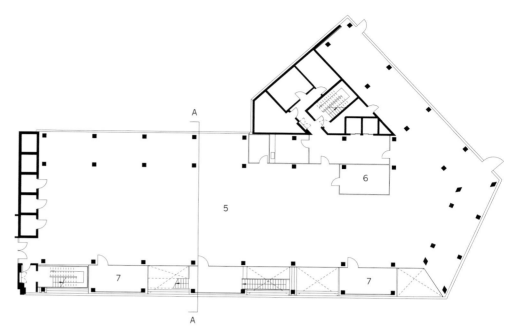

Typical floor plan

1 Entrance
2 Front desk
3 Multi-purpose space
4 Atrium
5 Office space
6 Meeting rooms
7 Open/closed lounge
8 Technical room

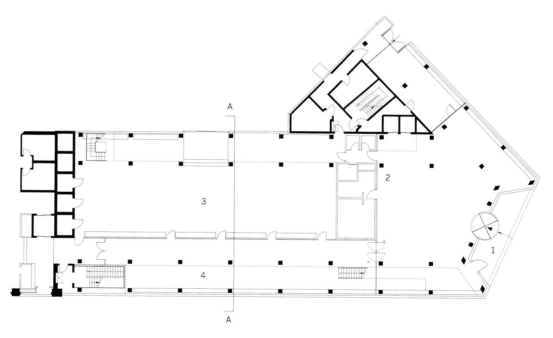

Ground floor plan

The structural timber frames were assembled on site. Once the frames were lifted into place, installation of floors and walls could begin.

Components combine to create a unique and expressive post-and-beam system.

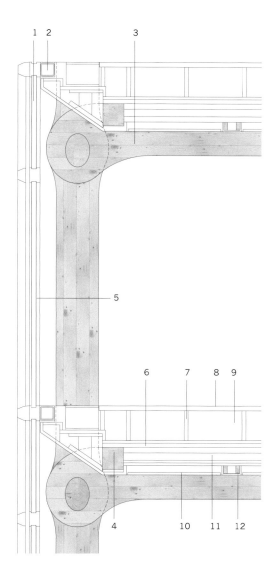

Detail section
1 External shading (fabric)
2 Steel square tube 140mm × 140mm
3 Laminated timber (spruce)
4 Wood joist 200mm × 267mm
5 Triple glazing
6 Three-layer wood board 45mm and mineral
  wool 60–160mm
7 Steel support for raised floor
8 Carpet and raised floor
9 Equipment installing space
10 Cooling/heating panel
11 Sand 80mm
12 Wood joist

The elements of the frame system were CNC-milled to create a precise 'kit of parts'. A full-size prototype was created and tested to refine the connection details and ensure that site assembly would proceed smoothly. The precision of CNC fabrication was critical to the success of this project. The wood to wood connections required great precision to achieve a tight fit; and the control of moisture content of the various wood components ensured that maximum performance would be realized over the service life of the building.

To comply with Swiss fire codes and provide the required fire resistance rating, all exposed structural members were oversized by 40mm in each direction. This creates a sacrificial charring layer that will protect and maintain the structural integrity of the building for the required one-hour duration when exposed to fire.

CONCLUSION
The Tamedia Head Office confirms the suitability of wood as a structural material in a high-performance office environment, where considerations of beauty and durability go hand in hand with the concern for ecology and occupant health. The success of this project both aesthetically and technically is the result of a highly sophisticated and seamlessly integrated approach to design and construction. The finely articulated structure with its curvilinear elements clearly illustrates the precision and expressive potential of digital fabrication. While the structural detailing of the building is unmistakably personal and may not lend itself to widespread replication, these underlying messages are readily transferable.

Details of precision CNC-milled components

CNC manufacturing: The CNC machine at Blumer-Lehmann AG enabled the production of a precise 'kit of parts.'
1 Glulam panel **2** 3D model of each piece is sent to CNC machine. **3** Large-scale CNC machine **4** Precise oval holes for the columns ensure an interlocking connection. **5** CNC machine is capable of five-axis rotation to produce angles. **6** Due to the diameter of the pieces a long milling bit was used. **7** Finished pieces are checked by hand before being shipped to the construction site. **8** Specialized undercut and high detail finishing is done by hand.

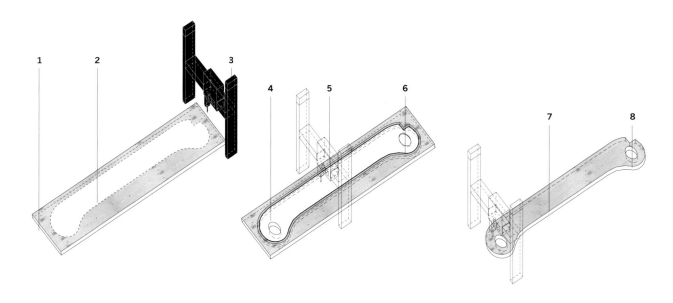

The joint configuration, combined with tapered diagonal members, enables the frame to resist twisting and bending.

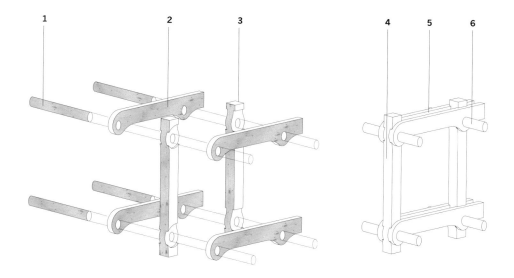

Joint assembly

1 CNC milled secondary oval beam **2** CNC milled primary beam **3** Interlocking column system **4** The column is locked into position by the beam grid **5** Primary beams distribute loads from the building **6** Oval beams lock the system in place and brace against shear forces.

Design concept

1 Existing Tamedia building **2** The mansard roof responds to the form of adjacent historic buildings. **3** Façade for extension over neighbouring building **4** Structural heavy timber frame **5** Façade for new construction **6** The entrance façade responds to the existing urban scale.

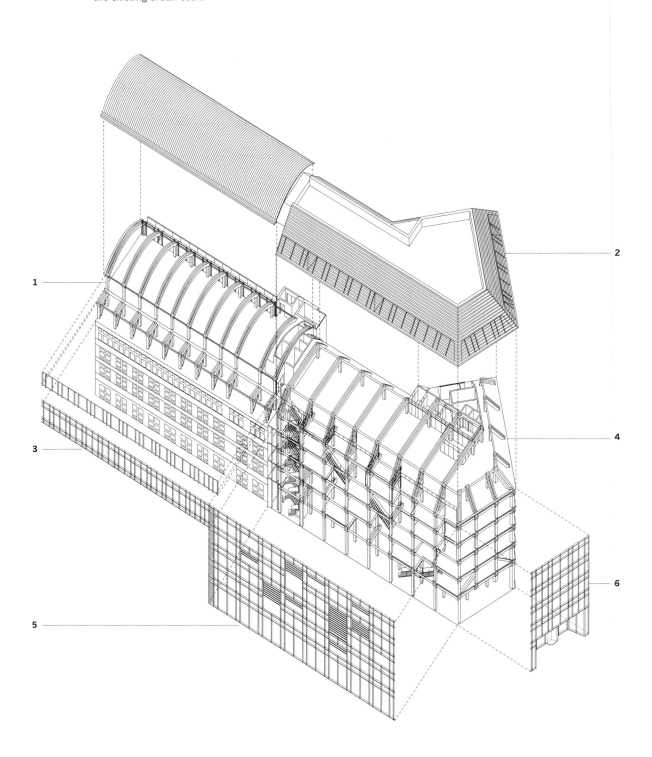

The building was designed with a double-envelope system, which reduces the energy required for heating and cooling. The intermediate space accommodates gathering areas and meeting rooms that complement the more traditional office space.

BULLITT CENTER

Seattle, USA [The Miller Hull Partnership]

2013	**Year**
The Bullitt Foundation/Point 32	**Client**
DCI Engineers	**Structural Engineer**
Calvert	**Engineered Wood Fabricator**
Schuchart	**Contractor**
Office	**Program**

A prototype commercial building designed for a 250-year service life, the Bullitt Center uses only as much energy as it can produce.

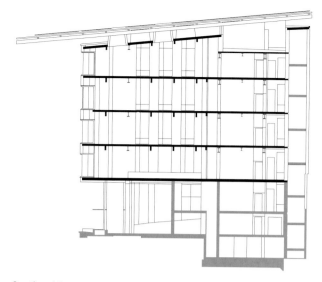

Section AA

The large photovoltaic canopy not only produces energy but also prevents the strong summer sun from entering the building.

The Bullitt Center features expansive views of downtown Seattle, the mountains and the ocean.

The Bullitt Foundation was established in Seattle, Washington, in 1952 by Dorothy Bullitt, a leading businesswoman and philanthropist, whose family had a long history in the establishment of civic and cultural institutions. In the 21st century, the Foundation's mission reflects the belief that in future, 'Sustainable human institutions and enterprises will be based on the same ecological principles that govern all ecosystems.'[1]

This new building houses the Bullitt Foundation offices on half of one floor, while the rest of the space is leased as office space to other tenants. With the goal of creating the world's 'greenest' commercial building, the Foundation chose to follow the principles of the Living Building Challenge (LBC), North America's most advanced green building rating system. To achieve LBC certification, buildings must meet a series of

performance imperatives, including the selection of a previously developed 'brownfield' site, 100% on-site renewable energy generation, 100% of water needs provided by harvested rainwater and on-site waste management.

CONCEPT

With a low surface-to-volume ratio, a high-performance building envelope, energy-efficient equipment and systems, and advanced daylighting strategies, the aim of the Bullitt Center was to reduce its operating energy demand by 80% relative to that of a traditionally constructed commercial building of the same size. This makes it possible for the building to be powered by a photovoltaic array that covers the full extent of the overhanging roof. In addition the building recycles its water and treats its own waste on site, and is con-

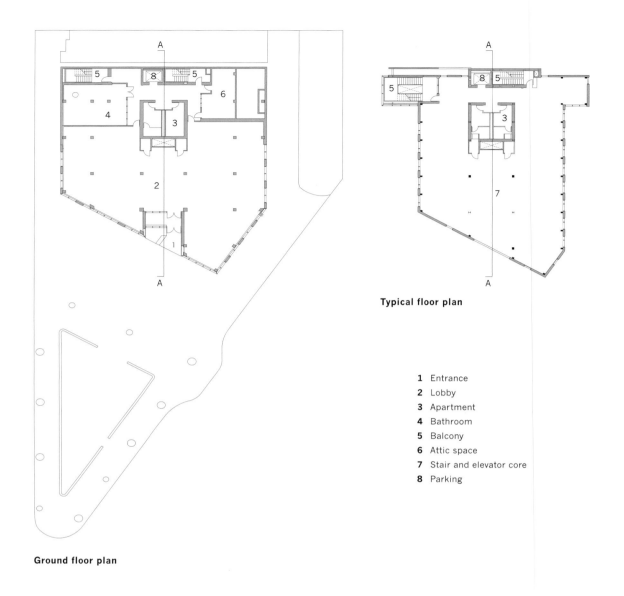

Ground floor plan

Typical floor plan

1 Entrance
2 Lobby
3 Apartment
4 Bathroom
5 Balcony
6 Attic space
7 Stair and elevator core
8 Parking

structed using durable, non-toxic materials that result in superior life cycle performance and interior environmental quality.

CONSTRUCTION

The six-storey, 4830 square metre podium structure includes two lower floors of concrete construction with four floors of heavy timber above. The choice of wood was not an immediate one; the architects initially believed the thermal mass of a concrete structure would be necessary to achieve the required energy performance. However, life cycle comparisons of various structural options concluded that timber would not compromise the goal of net zero energy, and at the same time offer additional aesthetic and environmental benefits. Wood could meet the durability require-

ments for the desired 250-year service life, reduce the need for potentially harmful interior finishes; and assist in meeting the carbon-neutral objectives of the project.

The wood structure comprises a glulam post-and-beam frame, with the floors and roof constructed of solid nail-laminated timber. This kind of wood structure was in common use for commercial buildings until the 1920s, but the Bullitt Center was the first to be built in Downtown Seattle for almost a century. The Douglas fir glulam columns and beams range in size from 130mm × 380mm to 310mm × 534mm. The nail-laminated timber decking is 2 × 6 inches (38mm × 140mm) for the floors and 2 × 4 inches (38mm × 89mm) for the roof. In accordance with the requirements of LBC, all the wood is sourced from

The nail-laminated floors provide additional structural rigidity.

The thermal mass of the concrete floors and the large high-performance windows are part of the sustainability strategy.

within a 1000 kilometer radius, and is Forest Steward-ship Council (FSC) certified.

For reasons of economy, it was necessary to specify industrial (rather than architectural) grade glulams, and to design simple connections that would be inexpensive to manufacture and quick to install. Rather than concealed knife plates, the design team devised a 'bucket' connection that could be attached to the columns, and would eliminate the need for temporary shoring of beams during erection.

Each glulam beam was cut to length on site, lifted by crane, set into the buckets and secured by screws. The choice of screws (rather than larger-diameter bolts) eliminated the need for pre-drilling and permitted the connection to be closer to the beam end, thus reducing the size of the buckets.

To avoid the effects of cumulative shrinkage that could result if the storey-height columns were allowed to bear on the floor beams, a steel tube spacer was in-stalled between the top of one column and the bottom of the column above. This detail isolates the effects of cross grain shrinkage in the floor beams at any given level to that individual storey.

The steel spacers also permit each floor beam to have approximately 75mm of direct bearing surface on the columns. Testing demonstrated that this approach offered an adequate measure of safety against structural collapse in case of fire, and it was therefore not necessary to protect the exposed steel connectors with intumescent paint. The structure is otherwise designed to provide the required resistance through the oversizing of members and the calculation of charring rate.

The City of Seattle supported the project, and offered flexibility in the interpretation of its own bylaws to assist in meeting the project goals. In one instance, the municipality agreed to relax the height limit for six-storey buildings to permit the floor-to-floor heights

Axonometric drawings of steel connections

Steel connection points within the structure resist seismic forces and reduced the construction time. **1** Glulam posts and beams are the main structural system on the top four floors. **2** Metal connection points join the columns and beams. The steel connectors bridge the small differences in the length of the beams. **3** Steel I-column **4** Steel I-beam **5** Chevron braces stiffen the building against lateral and seismic forces.

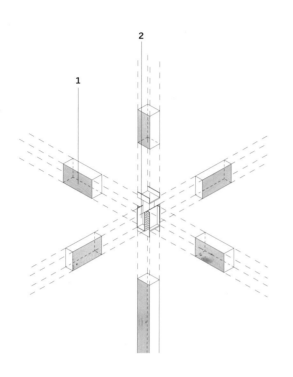

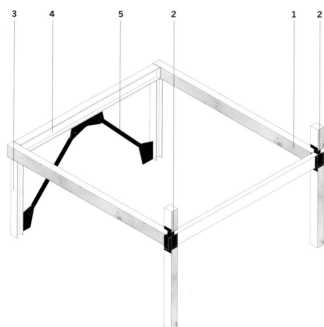

Construction sequence: A steel structure is used for the ground floor; glulam beams are connected to the steel structure; steel connections join columns and beam, and chevron braces provide additional strength.

The warmth of natural wood contributes to clean and comfortable working areas for a variety of building users.

to be raised to 4.7 metres. This was done to increase daylight penetration and reduce the energy required for artificial illumination, benefits that were further increased by the choice of a nail-laminated floor system. Much shallower than a conventional joisted floor, it also eliminated the need for perimeter beams, permitting the glazing to extend the full floor-to-ceiling height.

CONCLUSION

In its desire to catalyze market transformation, the Bullitt Foundation bore the cost of extensive research and development of this prototype urban commercial building. As the Foundation states:

'The goal of the Bullitt Center is to change the way buildings are designed, built and operated; to improve long-term environmental performance; and to promote broader implementation of energy efficiency, renewable energy and other green building technologies.'[2] While the Foundation's focus is the Pacific Northwest region of North America, the lessons learned from this project could have global implications.

REFERENCES

1   Denis Hayes, President and CEO, Bullitt Foundation, 2008.
2   The Bullitt Center: Retrieved from http://www.bullittcenter.org

WOOD INNOVATION AND DESIGN CENTRE

Prince George, Canada [MGA | Michael Green Architecture]

2014	**Year**
MJTST	**Client**
Equilibrium Consulting	**Structural Engineer**
Structurlam	**Engineered Wood Fabricator**
PCL	**Contractor**
Institutional/Office	**Program**

Foremost among many structural innovations, WIDC's staggered CLT floor system conceals service runs while permitting an exposed wood ceiling.

The entrance of WIDC is a two-storey open atrium, which features 355mm × 370mm glulam columns and 311mm × 570mm glulam beams. This post-and-beam system has end grain bearing columns for efficient and reliable transfer of forces through the structure.

The Wood Innovation and Design Centre (WIDC) was completed in October 2014. It is located in the centre of Prince George, the largest city in northern British Columbia, and an important centre for the province's forestry industry. The six-storey plus mechanical penthouse, 29.5 metre high structure was funded by the provincial government to demonstrate the immediate application and future potential of massive wood construction, serving as a showcase for local wood products and manufacturing processes.

CONCEPT

The Wood Innovation and Design Centre is the first Tall Wood building in Canada built beyond the area and height limitations of current building codes. With a mandate to push the limits of the material, WIDC incorporates wood wherever the building code and site-specific building regulation permit. This includes an innovative structural system using a range of locally manufactured, solid engineered wood products as well as a variety of interior and exterior wood finishes. The post-and-beam structural system creates long spans and flexible floor plates without the use of steel or concrete members. In fact, there is no concrete

used above the ground floor slab, with the exception of a concrete topping in the mechanical penthouse on the roof.

WIDC's main tenant will be the University of Northern British Columbia (UNBC), which will house its Master's degree programs in wood engineering and science on the first two and a half floors, accommodating research facilities, a lecture theatre and classrooms spaces. Offices of public and private sector organizations involved in the forestry industry will be located on the upper floors. Thus WIDC will serve as a gathering place for researchers, academics, design professionals and others interested in generating ideas for innovative uses of wood.

The form of the building is simple and elegant, allowing the beauty of wood to shine through. The exterior is inspired by bark peeling away from the trunk of a tree; thick and protective on the north side, thin and open on the south where the façade becomes more transparent to welcome passive solar heat gain. To the east and west, the wood columns supporting the curtain wall glazing cut the low angle of the rising and setting sun. The summer sun is controlled with wood slat blinds.

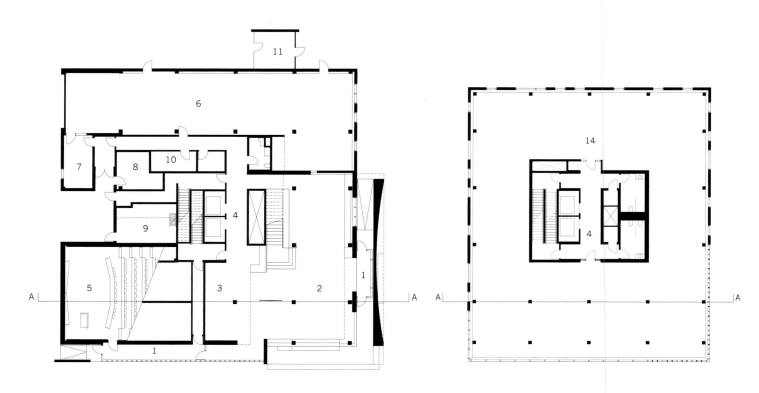

Ground floor plan

Typical floor plan

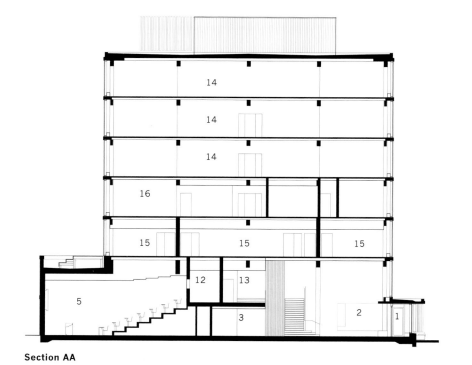

Section AA

1 Vestibule
2 Demonstration area
3 Cafe
4 Elevator lobby
5 Lecture theatre
6 Research lab below
7 Technician's office
8 Electrical services
9 Mechanical services
10 Garbage and recycling
11 Bike storage
12 Projection room
13 Mezzanine
14 Tenant space
15 Classroom
16 Office

View of lobby featuring LVL stairs and benches that enable its use as a gathering space for all the occupants of the building.

CONSTRUCTION

The design incorporates a simple, 'dry' structure of systems-integrated CLT (cross-laminated timber) floor panels, glulam columns and beams, and CLT walls. The wood structure is exposed as is the ceiling finish in most spaces. This simplicity translates into transferability and repeatability of the system. The floor consists of two layers of CLT panels running perpendicular to one another. On each layer, the CLT panels are spaced apart to create continuous cavities within the structural floor section that can accommodate services above and below, while enabling the upper and lower wood surfaces to be exposed. The upper panel

cavity is covered with a plywood panel. Spanning 6 metres between the post-and-beam frames, the wood-only floor system was selected to minimize the use of concrete and thus weight.

The choice to eliminate concrete from the floor assemblies and expose the structure created acoustic challenges. However, through extensive analysis and testing, the project team was able to achieve high-performing acoustic floors and partition walls and so meet the requirements of the BC Building Code. For the floors, an acoustically insulated subfloor system is loose-laid over the chases with cut-out panels to provide access to these floor trenches. Lighting and fire

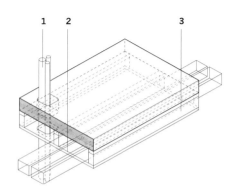
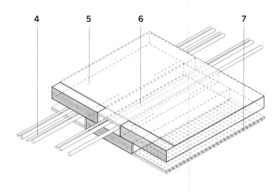

Diagram of floor systems

At WIDC (right), the staggered CLT floor system can accommodate the services within the structural depth, thus allowing for higher ceilings than would be possible with a joisted floor (left). **1** Services penetrate the floors vertically. **2** Ceiling chases provide space for services. **3** Dropped roof chases reduce ceiling heights in floors. **4** Services are run between the staggered floor panels. **5** Acoustic mats provide enhanced noise protection. **6** Easy access allows for adaptability and reuse within the building. **7** Acoustic paneling on the bottom of each chase allows for easy access and sound protection.

Construction sequence

WIDC had a tight time schedule. The elevator core was built from CLT panels and was assembled first, followed by the floor system. An innovative slab system allows for mechanical, electrical and water systems to be hidden with the floor slab. The chase system enables reconfiguration when needed by the client.

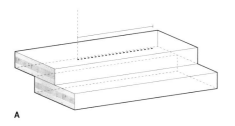
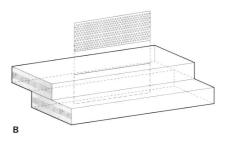
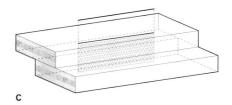

A   B   C

Assembly of floor system

A The CLT floor system is field-cut at specified spacings using a Mafell MKS 185 EC. The 750mm long plunge slot cuts through the upper and lower CLT panels, which allows for a precise and repeatable cut of the same depth. **B** Once the cuts have been made in the CLT floor system, the HSK mesh of 750mm long × 150mm deep is inserted into each cut. The HSK mesh has perforations at 50mm on centre. The HSK mesh is positioned with 75mm of its depth in the slot in the lower panel, and 75mm in the slot in the upper panel. **C** The channel is filled with a proprietary HSK epoxy that bonds the two panels together. The HSK epoxy system uses a pneumatically assisted applicator to ensure epoxy is delivered consistently throughout the channel.

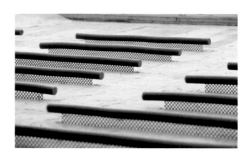
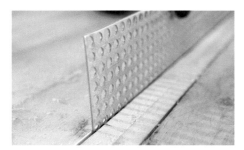

HSK connection system

The staggered five-ply and three-ply CLT panels were connected with a proprietary HSK connection that comprised a perforated metal plate installed in place with a field-cut slot through the panels where they intersect, and secured with an HSK epoxy adhesive. In addition to being more efficient and cost-effective than diagonal screws, the HSK connection system provides greater stiffness to the structural floor system.

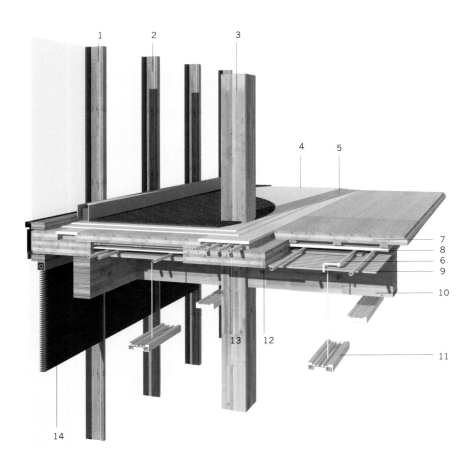

Diagram and section of floor construction

1 LVL curtain wall mullion
2 9mm carpet
3 Glulam column
4 7mm acoustic underlay
5 Two layers 13mm plywood
6 Sprinklers and services in ceiling trough
7 99mm three-layer CLT
8 Acoustic insulation
9 19mm × 38mm @ 75mm spacing wood, slats ceiling, black fabric, acoustic insulation
10 Glulam beam
11 Suspended light fixture
12 169mm five-layer CLT
13 Services in floor trough
14 Wood slat blinds
15 Service chase
16 50mm semi-rigid fibreglass board insulation
17 Sprinkler pipe, acoustic seal around penetration
18 Two layers 16mm gypsum wallboard
19 Two layers 25mm semi-rigid fibreglass board insulation
20 Curtain wall, aluminum veneer, LVL mullion, triple glazing

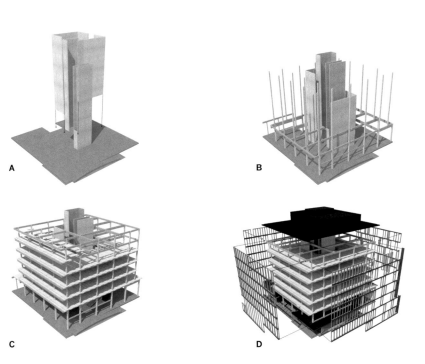

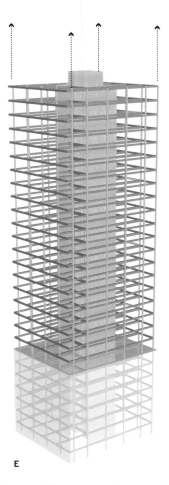

A The lateral load resistance is primarily provided by the elevator and stair core walls, which consist of CLT panels. These shear walls are anchored to the foundations using a combination of shear brackets and hold-down anchors. B Concealed proprietary aluminum dovetail. Pitzl connectors are used to join the beams and columns of the glulam frame. C Staggered CLT floor panels are installed. Upper floor columns bear directly on columns from the floor below. LVL wind columns and SIPs were then used on each floor. D The building envelope with curtain wall glazing and wood cladding is set in place, and the building is then topped by the roof with a mechanical penthouse. Services and interior partitions are installed. E The structural system used for WIDC has been proven as a structural concept for commercial buildings up to 30 storeys.

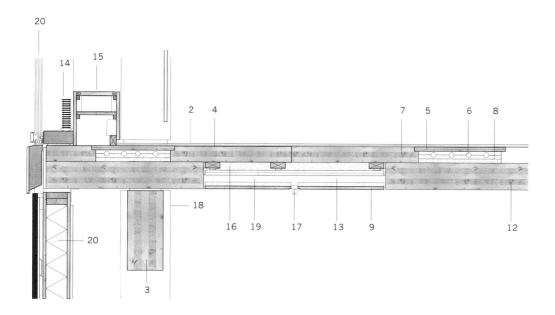

The HSK connection system allows for concealed services in floor and ceiling assemblies. It also enables acoustic separation and flexibility for fitting out for future tenant finishes and services.

View of east elevation. LVL columns support the curtain wall glazing.

suppression systems are run in the ceiling recesses, concealed with a simple, removable wood-slat finish. The acoustic performance of the floor assembly is further improved by a noise-barrier system lining the underside of the top CLT within the ceiling chase. The service chases inherent in the structural system offer flexibility for future reconfiguration. Therefore, the need for secondary ceiling finishes to conceal service runs is significantly reduced. Additional acoustic measures were required to increase the acoustic performance of the lecture theatre, both in terms of sound isolation from adjacent spaces and for speech intelligibility within the room.

Rather than protecting the wood structure from exposure to fire by covering it with non-combustible material, the wood is left exposed, and fire resistance was demonstrated through computer modelling and calculations. The massive timber will char slowly enough to provide the required fire protection. The most vulnerable parts of the system in a fire are in fact the steel connectors between massive timber elements. All connectors are therefore set into and protected by the timber.

CONCLUSION

The Wood Innovation and Design Centre was the subject of a detailed life cycle impact analysis comparing the wood solution with a hypothetical alternative built in concrete. The environmental performance of the wood building was superior in all respects, most nota-

bly: in its potential impact on global warming (88% improvement); non-renewable energy consumption (43% improvement); acidification (47% improvement); and ozone depletion (54% improvement).[1]

This project has set many precedents in the North American building context through the extensive engineering research and testing undertaken by the project team to prove the safety and reliability of massive timber construction. As the example of WIDC is followed elsewhere on the continent, North American building codes will no doubt respond, and recognize Tall Wood construction as a standard, safe practice.

REFERENCES

1   Athena Sustainable Materials Institute (2015) New Environmental Building Declaration for WIDC. Retrieved from http://www. athenasmi.org/news-item/new-environmental-building-declaration-for-widc/

The main entrance canopy comprises two LVL slabs supported on a colonnade of Alaskan yellow cedar. The clear glazing at the entrance provides a visual connection to the demonstration area.

HYBRID SYSTEMS

In addition to satisfying the requirements of program, structural design is also concerned with efficiency and economy of means. In some cases, a pure wood frame or panel structure may not provide the optimal solution.

Hybrid systems, in which different materials and structural solutions are used in combination, are common. The choice may be made for architectural, structural, environmental or economic reasons, or because of local construction practices or code requirements. The examples documented in this section opted for the following solutions:

The floor system for the Badenerstrasse Mixed-Use Building consists of prefabricated LVL panels, whereas the walls use closely spaced green timber posts, a solution designed to minimize carbon footprint and ensure recyclability.

LCT One uses a simple system of wood/concrete composite floor panels, and prefabricated wall panels incorporating glulam columns, a combination that speeds up the erection process and minimizes use of material.

The Wenlock Mixed-Use Building has a concrete ground floor and circulation core, with a steel frame superstructure creating cantilevers that articulate the façade, and CLT panels for walls and floors.

The Treet Apartment Building has a perimeter structure of glulam trusses, CLT stair and elevator cores and hybrid glulam and concrete 'power' floors that support stacked modular apartment units.

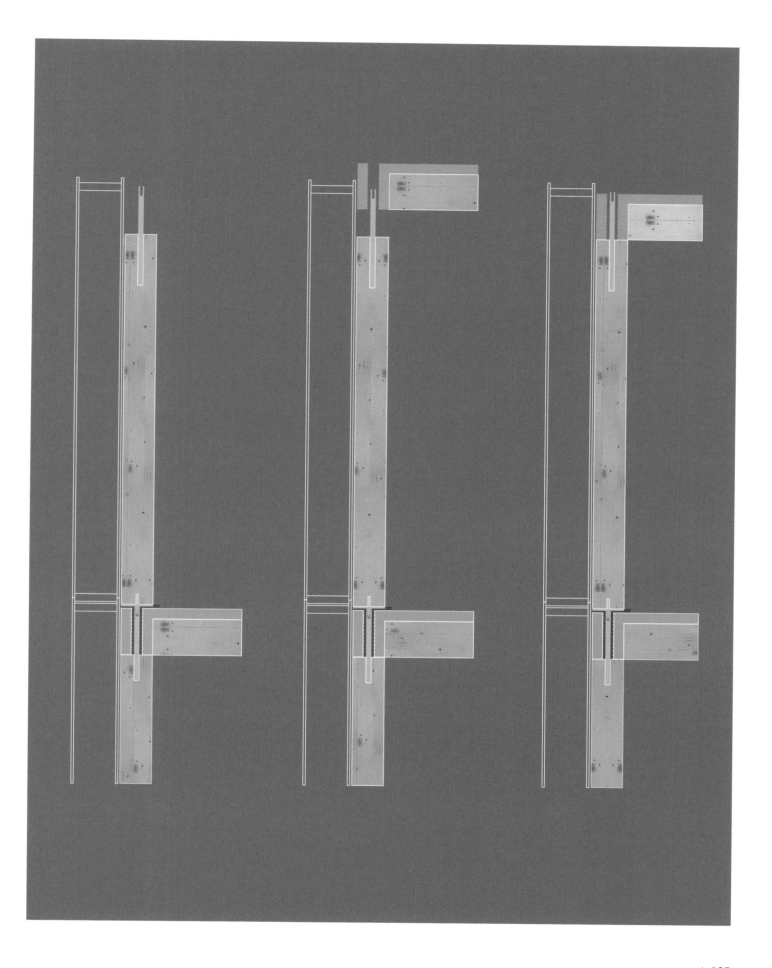

BADENERSTRASSE MIXED-USE BUILDING

Zurich, Switzerland [Pool Architekten]

2010	**Year**
Baugenossenschaft Zurlinden	**Client**
SJB Kempter Fitze AG	**Structural Engineer**
Zimmereigenossenschaft Zürich	**Engineered Wood Fabricator**
Caretta Weidmann AG	**Contractor**
Residential/Commercial	**Program**

The Badenerstrasse project questions current assumptions
about the use of wood in contemporary buildings,
and offers a low-tech vision of a sustainable future.

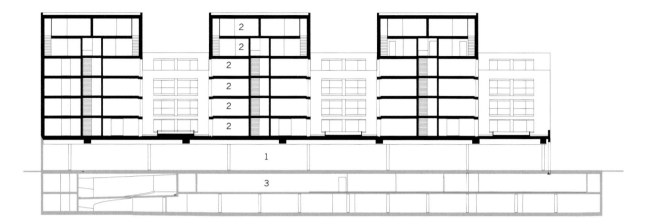

Section AA

Located in central Zurich, this project is the first in Switzerland to meet the requirements of new energy regulations based on the criteria of the 2000 Watt Society.[1] The building extends the full depth of the property between Badenerstrasse and the new Hardau city park. The mixed-use program includes retail space occupying a single-storey concrete podium, above which are 54 apartments spread over six storeys, and constructed using field-assembled massive timber panels.

CONCEPT

Above the podium, the residential accommodation is divided into six contiguous rectangles, alternately pushed forward toward the park, or back toward Badenerstrasse. The result is that both main façades are strongly articulated as a series of vertical volumes separated by courtyards.

All units are arranged in linear fashion and extend the full depth of the building. This allows for through ventilation, natural light from multiple directions and the opportunity to create a more 'closed' elevation toward the busy street, and a more open one toward the park. Balconies on the park side further articulate the vertical massing and connect the building and its occupants visually to the surroundings. Building entrances are located on both sides, strengthening connections to the immediate neighbourhood and animating the public realm.

The façade is clad in fibre cement panels, which give the building an impression of massiveness appropriate to its city centre setting. As such, it sits comfortably among its historic neighbours, most of which have stucco or stone façades.

CONSTRUCTION

The six apartment storeys are constructed using a simple cross wall structure that remains consistent throughout the height of the building. Wood construction offered numerous advantages. In addition to the shortened construction schedule that results from the use of prefabricated and modular elements, wood offered reduced weight and environmental attributes consistent with the project goals.

Badenerstrasse is the first project to use the 'Top Wall' system developed by the Swiss engineer and carpenter Hermann Blumer as the main structural support system. The system is based on standardized 100mm × 200mm spruce wood vertical supports that do not need to be kiln-dried to perform effectively. The elements are not factory-prefabricated into wall panel units (as is usual in contemporary massive timber construction), but instead positioned and fixed in

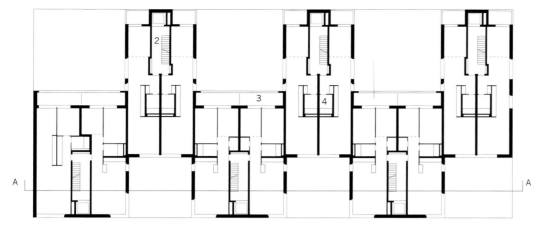

1   Supermarket
2   Stairwell
3   Balcony
4   Elevator shaft

Typical floor plan

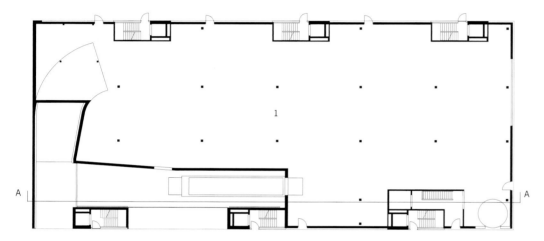

Ground floor plan

place on sleepers, using 20mm diameter beech wood dowels or plug anchors inserted into pre-drilled holes. The floors are a prefabricated panelized construction, consisting of 40mm upper and lower skins of laminated veneer lumber with 160mm deep joists, the voids being filled with a 50mm layer of gravel. Above the panel is a 30mm layer of sound insulation, covered with 70mm of concrete screed (including in-floor radiant heating), and a finish floor. Below the panel resilient channels are mounted, with a gypsum fibreboard finish.

With the introduction of digital fabrication, building with massive timber has become a high-tech, high-precision method of construction. In contrast, the approach taken in this project (particularly with respect to the walls) is intentionally low-tech. Here, the natural properties and variability of wood as an organic mate-

rial are accepted and incorporated into the system. Two aspects are of particular interest.

Firstly, the vertical elements are configured with a 10mm gap between them, which allows the wood to shrink, swell or warp perpendicular to grain. While the elements are precise in the vertical dimension, this configuration allows for a 5% change in the size of the cross section. It is not necessary to process the material to avoid knots and splits, as these do not affect the overall performance of the system.

Secondly, because the wood used is not processed, glued or nailed, it can be easily dismantled and reclaimed at full structural value, when it reaches the end of its initial service life. Thus the material can be incorporated into other high-quality wooden products, as was common practice with reclaimed timbers well into the first half of the 20th century.

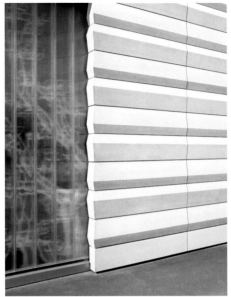

The breathable cement cladding is the outermost layer of a highly insulated vapour-permeable wall construction.

A worker installs the horizontal pegs that connect the posts into a continous wall.

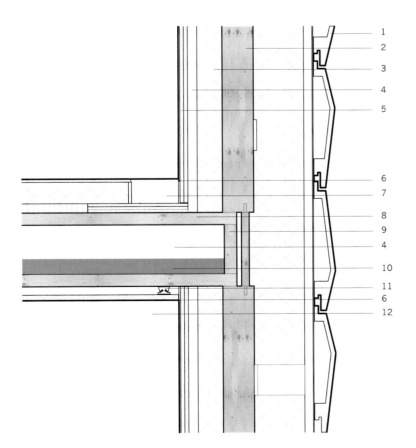

Detail section

1 Breathable cement cladding
2 Solid spruce 'Top Wall' system
3 Insulation cavity on both sides of the solid wood posts
4 Ventilated cavity
5 Double layer of gypsum fibreboard
6 Acoustic spacer
7 Utility cavity
8 OSB panel
9 Beech wood Rawl plug
10 Acoustic insulation
11 Acoustic ceiling hanger
12 Gypsum ceiling

Non-load-bearing walls within the building consist of wood and metal elements depending on the service systems running through them.

Wall prior to application of gypsum board. Notice the metal brackets used to stabilize and connect sections of the wall to the floor beneath.

With the wood posts at its core, the exterior wall construction includes 80mm of mineral fibre insulation, 30mm strapping, felt and gypsum fibreboard to the inside; and house wrap, 160mm mineral fibre insulation, 30mm battens and 70mm fibre cement rainscreen cladding to the outside.

With respect to Zurich's new energy performance requirements, the norms stipulated by SIA Effizienzpfad Energie (Path toward Energy Efficiency)[2] were the basis for the calculation of the operational and embodied energy to optimize both the construction methods and the performance of the building. The choice of a construction system based on solid sawn lumber significantly reduced the embodied energy of the building. Energy for building operation is supplied by a heat pump, solar panels and the recycling of heat produced by the supermarket on the ground floor.

CONCLUSION

The Badenerstrasse project not only expands our understanding of contemporary approaches to sustainable building, questioning some current assumptions and preconceptions, but also anticipates a future in which resource shortages will make the recycling and reuse of buildings and building materials an industry imperative.

REFERENCES

1   The 2000 Watt Society is a model, first developed by ETH Zurich, that aims to reduce energy consumption to a continuous 2000 Watts per capita, the level it believes is necessary to achieve long-term stabilization of the Earth's climate.

2   "Merkblatt SIA Effizienzpfad Energie" (SIA 2040), 2011. http://www.sia.ch/de/themen/energie/effizienzpfad-energie/

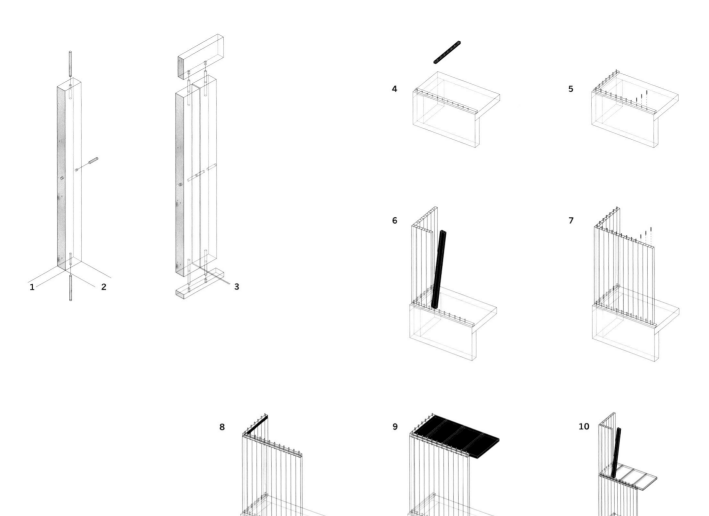

Drawing of 'Top Wall' system

1 100mm solid green spruce posts **2** 200mm width **3** Wall posts are separated by 10mm to allow for shifting and swelling within the wall. **4** Wood supports with regular holes provide the base for the wall system. **5** Wooden dowels are inserted into the holes and secure each post in the wall. **6** Each post is placed onto its own peg and horizontal pegs connect the posts. **7** Dowels are inserted into the top of the posts and hold the next wooden support layer.
8 The support layer holds the next wall layer and frames the floor.
9 Wooden floor panels are placed on the wooden posts. **10** The process starts again to build the next floor.

The 'Top Wall' system before and during construction. The pegs are already inserted and the posts are about to be installed.

LCT ONE

Dornbirn, Austria [Architekten Hermann Kaufmann]

2012	**Year**
Cree GmbH, a division of the Rhomberg Group	**Client**
Merz Kley Partner Zt GmbH	**Structural Engineer**
Sohm HolzBautechnik GmbH	**Engineered Wood Fabricator**
Cree GmbH, a division of the Rhomberg Group	**Contractor**
Office	**Program**

In this example of contemporary craftsmanship, the detailing of components informs the overall design, the result being a compelling combination of poetry and pragmatism.

The entrance and lobby display the glulam columns and beams. The lobby also acts as a small research area that allows visitors to understand the principles of construction of LCT One.

Located in the Austrian federal state of Vorarlberg and completed in 2012, Life Cycle Tower (LCT) One draws on the architectural tradition of the region. Isolated for centuries by mountainous topography, Vorarlberg developed a craft-based approach to wood building that combined efficiency, economy and elegance. Updated to embrace high-precision digital manufacturing, the careful detailing of wood structures remains a central driver of contemporary design.

CONCEPT

With a gross floor area of 2300 square metres and a height of eight storeys, LCT One was conceived as a prototype for a new approach to building that could greatly reduce the carbon footprint and environmental impact of urban development and redevelopment around the world. Supported by Regionalentwicklung Vorarlberg, an association of municipalities, professional and technical organizations, the building is the result of a two-phase study led by Creative Resource

and Energy Efficiency (Cree), a division of the Rhomberg Group. Phase 1 (known as '8+' and conducted in collaboration with architect Michael Schluder) confirmed the technical viability of high-rise construction in wood; Phase 2 refined the initial concept into a hybrid solution that could compete with standard concrete construction for buildings up to 30 storeys. Designed as a commercial office, LCT One uses a highly systematized, yet highly flexible hybrid solid wood and concrete post, beam and panel system. Before embarking on the detailed design of LCT One, the project team made a conceptual application to the approving authority. Permission for the project was granted in principle, subject to the design meeting certain provisions, specifically in regard to structural fire protection. With the exception of the cast-in-place concrete stair tower (required by the approving authority), the building is made entirely from factory-prefabricated wall and floor components, which reduced on-site construction time to only eight days.

The carefully proportioned wall panel system gives the building a simple and elegant appearance.

1 Entrance
2 Demonstration area
3 Office areas
4 Concrete core
5 Concrete pad

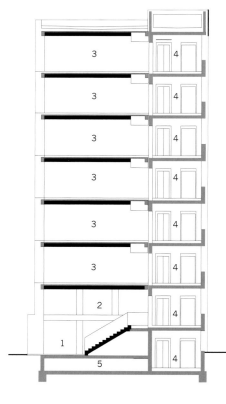

CONSTRUCTION

Conceptually, LCT One is constructed from a 'kit' of only three parts: load-bearing exterior columns, floor panels that span between the columns and the concrete stair core, and exterior wall panels to enclose the building. In practice, the system was reduced to two parts, with the columns being built into the exterior wall panels.

The choice of a glulam frame rather than a load-bearing CLT panel system for the vertical structure was driven by the desire to optimize material use. Unlike CLT, where alternate laminations are perpendicular to one another, the grain in glulam is all oriented in a single direction. This makes it highly efficient for carrying vertical loads and, with end grain bearing, eliminates the issue of moisture-related shrinkage.

LCT One uses paired glulam columns, each 240mm × 240mm, separated by a 10mm gap. The columns are sized to achieve 90-minute fire resistance, and the column pairs are spaced at 2.7 metres centres. The floor-to-floor height in LCT One is 3.3 metres, but the system can be adapted to any required floor height. The wood/concrete composite floor panels measure 2.7 × 8.1 metres and consist of four 240mm × 280mm glulam beams with an 80mm thick concrete slab, cast as a coffer with down-stands on the short sides. The choice of concrete increased the thermal mass of the building, improved acoustic performance

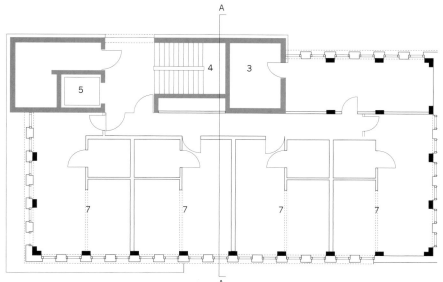

Typical floor plan

1 Entrance
2 Demonstration area
3 Storage and WC
4 Stairs
5 Elevator
6 Storage
7 Office areas

Ground floor plan

Installation of panels

1 Hybrid floor panel placed on top of wall panel. **2** A full wall panel is lowered into place using the steel tubes as guides. **3** Once the panel is in place, it is temporarily secured. **4** A non-shrink grout is placed around the steel tube and allowed to dry, creating a secure and fireproof assembly. **5** A crane is used to place the next hybrid floor panel, using the holes in the four corners. **6** Once the floor panel is in place, the workers can move to the next storey and repeat the process. Each floor requires approximately one day to complete.

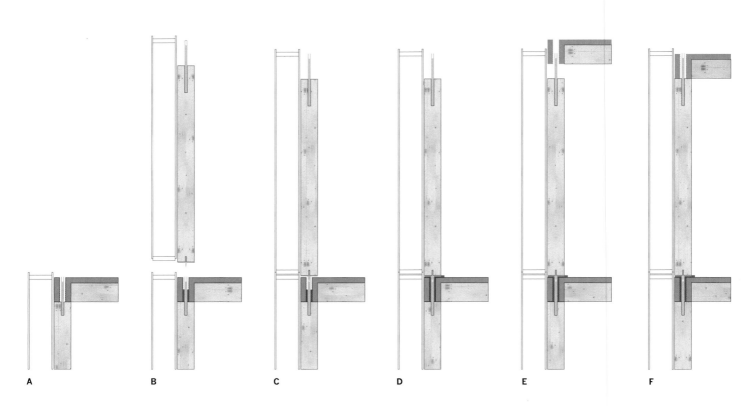

A   B   C   D   E   F

LCT One uses prefabricated panels that allow construction to move at a rate of one floor per day. The construction sequence shows the installation of panels.

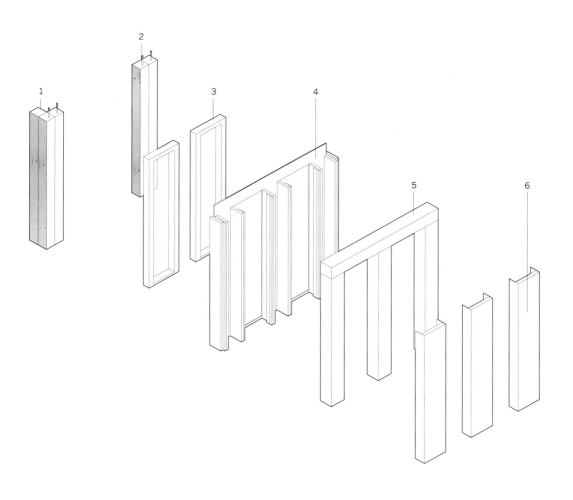

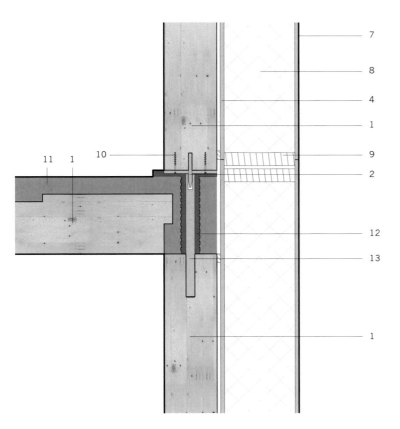

**Diagram and detail section
of wall construction**

1 Glulam column
2 Steel connection point
3 Window frames
4 OSB panel
5 Concrete floor
6 Aluminum façade
7 Cement-bonded chipboard
8 Insulation
9 Dimensional wood member
10 Steel plate connection point
11 Concrete floor topping
12 Non-shrink grout
13 Steel tube

1

2

3

Hybrid floor system

1 The panels went through rigourous fire-proofing tests. The concrete top layer shields the upper floors from fire, thus allowing occupants time to escape. **2** Digital fabrication techniques for wall panels and the hybrid floor system resulted in a high degree of precision. **3** Services can be accommodated beside the beams and are then hidden by heating and cooling panels (chilled beams) that fit in between the beams.

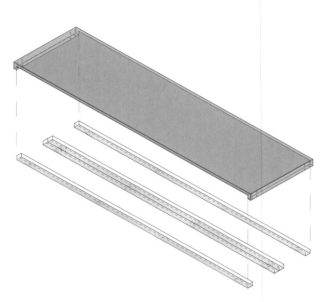

Once the glulam beams are arranged, a mold is created and concrete is poured into the mold. The factory setting yields a high degree of accuracy. Each floor panel is made to within 10mm of the size that was needed.

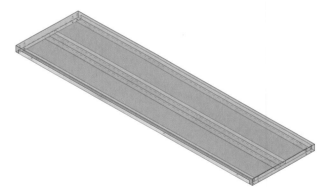

The floor panels have holes cut out in each one of the corners to facilitate each panel to be slipped into place; the floor and wall system can be joined with a high degree of precision.

Construction sequence

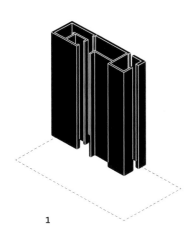

1

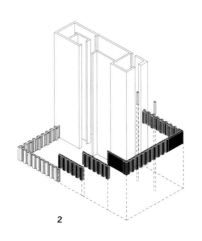

2

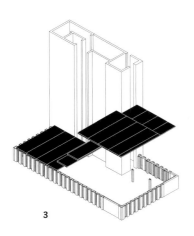

3

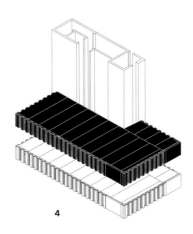

4

1 The concrete base and elevator/stair core is poured to the full height of the building. This provides structural support and bracing for the wooden component system. **2** In large sections, the prefabricated wall panels are placed either onto the base concrete pad, or onto one of the floor panels of the wood/concrete hybrid floor system. **3** The hybrid floor system has holes in each of the four corners for rapid placement. **4** Each floor takes approximately one day to complete, thus resulting in a very short construction time for the entire building.

Interior with all panels installed. The space is free from columns or obstructions, services are run through floor and wall panels and the floor can be customized for the individual occupant.

and provided the fire separation between storeys that was required by the approving authority.

The slabs were cast in the prefabrication shop, reducing tolerances from the 12mm required for site concrete work, to less than 1mm. This technique also eliminated wet trades from the building site, reducing construction time and minimizing the possibility of moisture damage to the wood components.

The slabs have circular holes cast into each corner, which engage steel tubes that are factory-fitted to the tops of the glulam posts. The resulting connection is filled with non-shrink grout. By creating a non-combustible platform between each storey-height column and the next, the design meets the approving authority's requirement for fire separation between floors. Steel plates and bolts connect the beam ends to the supporting columns, and the edge beams of adjacent panels together. This creates a diaphragm that transfers lateral loads to the concrete stair core. All interior partitions are non-load-bearing.

The coffers created by the floor system run from the perimeter of the building to the stair core. These coffers accommodate prefabricated service units that contain electrical, mechanical, fire suppression and other systems that connect into vertical service risers in the core. The concrete slab and down-stand beams create a non-combustible lining for the concealed service spaces. Raised floors accommodate additional services and reduce the transfer of structure-borne noise from one floor to another.

Because the external walls are non-load-bearing, they could have been fully glazed. However in LCT One, these walls are framed and sheathed, using engineered wood studs and OSB panels, and have punched

LCT One houses the offices of Cree GmbH.

window openings. This enabled the glulam posts to be built into the walls, a technique that simplified site assembly and further reduced construction time. The panels were supplied to site fully insulated to Passive House standard and with exterior sheathing already attached. However, to minimize the possibility of damage during transportation, the aluminum cladding was installed on site. Each storey consists of five wall panels and nine floor panels, with each taking only a few minutes to install. As a result, each floor took only five hours to complete, including the grouting of connections and the sealing of the exterior envelope.

CONCLUSION
Through the optimization of materials, the design and construction of LCT One achieved a 50% reduction in resource use and a 90% reduction in carbon emissions compared to standard concrete frame construction. Carbon-neutral construction would have been theoretically possible if the concrete stair core had been replaced with a CLT core. Aesthetically, the precise detailing of components and their careful assembly into a coherent structural system gives LCT One a rational yet elegant architectural language.

17–21 WENLOCK ROAD MIXED-USE BUILDING

London, England [Hawkins\Brown]

2015	**Year**
Regal Homes	**Client**
Pringuer-James Consulting Engineers (concrete); Engenuity (timber and steel)	**Structural Engineer**
Binderholz	**Engineered Wood Fabricator**
B&K Structures	**Contractor**
Residential/Commercial	**Program**

A hybrid wood, concrete and steel construction was the most efficient solution for the offset geometry of this structure, in which the cruciform plan ensures good daylight and cross ventilation for each apartment.

Many apartments have views over the adjacent park, each given a different character by the shifting plan geometry.

1 Entrance
2 Car lift to underground parking
3 Amenity space
4 Apartment

Section AA

This ten-storey mixed-use building, includes ground floor commercial space with 50 apartment units above. The project is located next to the historic Regent's Canal in the London Borough of Hackney. The borough has been an early supporter of massive timber construction, having been the approving authority for both the Murray Grove (2009) and Bridport House (2012) projects.

Long one of London's poorest boroughs, Hackney is now in the process of renewal, as a new generation of residents choose it for its proximity to central London and the recreational amenities offered by the canal, its towpath and the nearby Olympic legacy park. With its mix of social and market housing, the project at 17–21 Wenlock Road can be seen as emblematic of this transition.

CONCEPT

In London, medium-density housing projects such as this have tended toward a standard typology, with two opposing blocks of apartments facing a linear courtyard. This configuration is rarely optimal for natural light and ventilation, responds poorly to the immediate urban context and provides only undifferentiated communal outdoor space.

The project team wanted to address all these shortcomings and devised a cruciform plan by which each apartment could be assured of dual exposure that would afford better access to daylight and cross ventilation. The arms of the plan would in turn define four smaller courtyards, with different orientations and different characters. To emphasize views up and down the canal and to individualize the apartments, the plan is rotated on the rectangular site, and successive floors are offset from one another, creating generous balconies.

CONSTRUCTION

When the London Borough of Hackney granted planning permission in 2012, it set a precedent by requir-

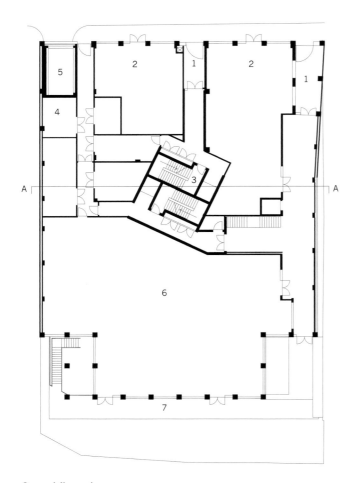

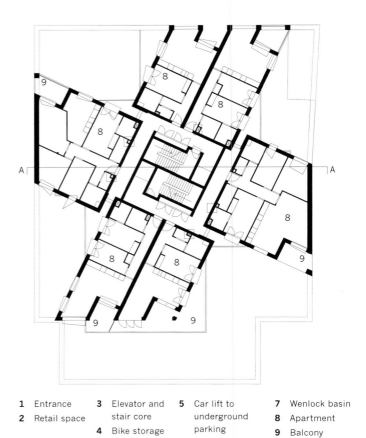

Ground floor plan

Typical floor plan

1	Entrance	**3**	Elevator and	**5**	Car lift to	**7**	Wenlock basin
2	Retail space		stair core		underground	**8**	Apartment
		4	Bike storage		parking	**9**	Balcony
				6	Amenity space		

The western red cedar façade provides a durable and longlasting finish for the building. The geometry of the building creates four courtyards, each with a different character.

The cruciform plan rotates incrementally as its moves upwards.

ing that the project be constructed using CLT. While this requirement was in keeping with the Borough's own environmental philosophy and anticipatory of emerging market demand, it nonetheless posed some technical challenges.

The architects had previously used CLT in a large low-rise school project, and recognized that the material lends itself best to load-bearing structural systems when walls are superimposed on one another and hence load paths are straightforward. Given the offset geometry of the proposed building, hybrid systems were investigated. The one that offered the greatest economy and flexibility incorporated all three of the major construction materials – concrete, steel and wood.

The basement parking garage and ground floor commercial space are constructed in reinforced concrete, above which extends a concrete stair and elevator core that provides all the required resistance to lateral loads. Around this core is a steel frame consisting of hollow square section (HSS) interior columns and

beams. At the perimeter of the building, where the frame must carry the loads of the external walls, universal (I-section) columns and beams are used. This outer frame is capable of transferring the vertical load of the exterior walls and supporting the necessary cantilevers for the balconies, enabling CLT panels to be used as non-load-bearing infill.

The floors are made from 200mm thick CLT panels, as are the exterior and interior walls enclosing each suite. Wood frame interior partitions reduce the overall weight of the building and offer residents the possibility of reconfiguring their suite in future if desired. Local fire regulations made encapsulation the most straightforward and predictable approach to achieve the 90-minute fire resistance required for a building of this size and type. All CLT surfaces are therefore covered with two layers of gypsum wallboard, and steel components are treated with intumescent paint.

In the absence of well-developed noise abatement standards for CLT construction, a prototype apartment was built on the ground floor and testing was carried

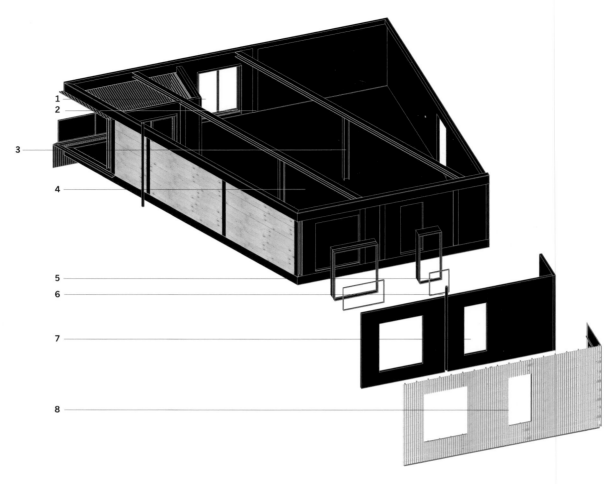

Building composition
1 Steel members brace and stabilize CLT panels. **2** Interior walls are CLT panels. **3** Floors and roofs are CLT panels. **4** Floors and walls are CLT panels. **5** Tilt and turn windows **6** Metal balustrades **7** Insulation with drainage runs hidden behind cladding. **8** External rain screen: timber cladding in western red cedar

out before construction details were finalized. It was found that the encapsulation strategy for fire protection also addressed the issues of noise transmission, so no additional acoustic treatment was required. The use of prefabricated panels into which door and window openings were already cut, made for quick, quiet construction, which greatly reduced the disruption to neighbours on a tight urban site. Externally the building is clad in western red cedar slats while a masonry screen wall facing the street gives the building a strong urban presence in keeping with its industrial context.

CONCLUSION
The Wenlock Road project is an innovative departure from traditional multi-family residential typologies that embodies both passive design strategies and a hybrid structure with lower embodied energy. By addressing new legislative imperatives in a creative yet pragmatic way, Wenlock Road responds to the emerging market demand for higher-quality design and environmentally conscious construction.

The hybrid **CLT** and steel structural system uses steel beams and columns of varying sizes for the primary structure and CLT panels for roofs, floors and walls. As the steel structure is erected, the CLT panels are connected by L-brackets.

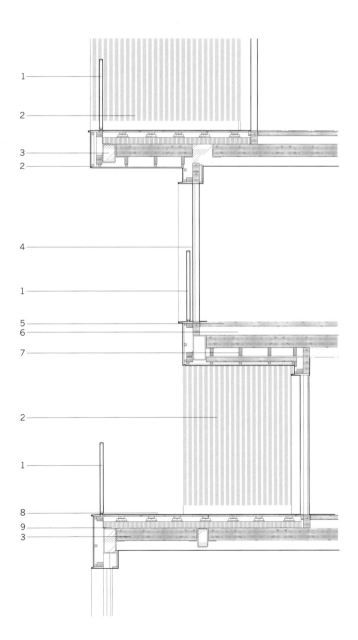

Detail section

1. External balustrade
2. Untreated western red cedar cladding
3. HSS steel
4. Inward-opening tilt and turn composite window set
5. Internal flooring
6. Insulation
7. Joist hanger
8. Red cedar on raised pedestal system
9. CLT panel

TREET APARTMENT BUILDING

Bergen, Norway [Artec Arkitekter]

2015	**Year**
Bergen og Omegn Boligbyggelag	**Client**
Sweco	**Structural Engineer**
Moelven; Kodumaja	**Engineered Wood Fabricator**
Residential	**Program**

The glulam truss structure of this 49 metre tall tower creates a series of horizontal racks on which modular apartment units are stacked.

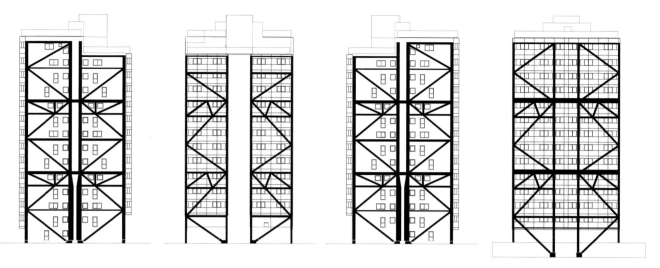

The structural system of glulam beams and columns is built in five-storey increments. At each five-storey level a concrete powerdeck distributes the weight of the modules into the vertical glulam truss structure.

Norway has a long and celebrated tradition of building in wood. Most famous are its elaborate 12th and 13th century stave churches, 28 of which still survive. Their internal structure of tall timber posts and lateral cross bracing enabled some of these churches to attain heights in excess of 20 metres. Nowadays, Norwegian architects and engineers use glulams to create large and long-span structures, including sports halls and bridges with spans up to 100 metres.

In 2012, Bergen og Omegn Boligbyggelag (BOB), a large and influential Norwegian housing association, declared its intention to commission the world's tallest timber residential building. Having identified a prominent site on the Bergen waterfront, BOB began to assemble a team capable of delivering such a project. The result was Treet (Norwegian for 'The Tree'), a 14-storey tower containing 62 apartments, whose glulam truss structure draws its inspiration from contemporary bridge design.

CONCEPT

The structural system for Treet mimics that used previously by Sweco on a five-storey building in Trondheim (2005), which had been further developed for an unrealized 20-storey project in Kirkenes. The concept is analogous to that of a cabinet rack filled with drawers, in which the sides and shelves of the rack are formed by large glulam trusses, and the drawers consist of prefabricated residential modules. Research

and testing of the dynamic performance and fire resistance of the structure was carried out with the assistance of the Norwegian University of Science and Technology, and Innovation Norway.

The building is rectangular in plan, measuring approximately 21 × 23 metres. Although contained within this rectangle, the CLT stair and elevator shafts are independent of the main structure. The entire building is then enclosed in a weatherproof envelope, with fully glazed façades on the north and south and opaque metal cladding on the east and west.

CONSTRUCTION

Poor soil conditions dictated the requirement for an extensive piled foundation, which has been tied together with a single-storey concrete parking garage structure that forms a podium for the building.

A structure of this size is subject to substantial lateral forces, and the glulam truss and bracing elements are connected using a system of embedded steel plates and pins originally developed for the roof of the speed skating oval constructed for the Olympic Winter Games in Lillehammer in 1994. In addition to diagonal braces on the façades, the structure is stiffened by two 'power storeys' (the shelves of the cabinet rack) located at levels five and ten.

These 'power storeys' comprise a grid of storey-height trusses that also serve to support precast concrete floors. The weight of the concrete improves the load

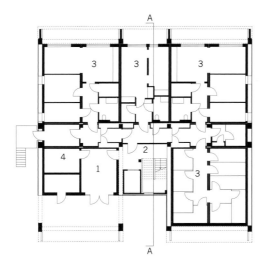

Ground floor plan

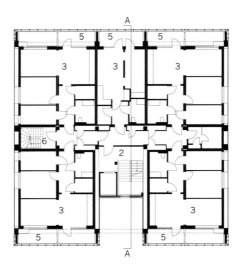

Typical floor plan

1 Entrance
2 Stair/elevator core
3 Apartments
4 Storage
5 Balcony
6 Stairwell
7 Gym
8 Concrete basement

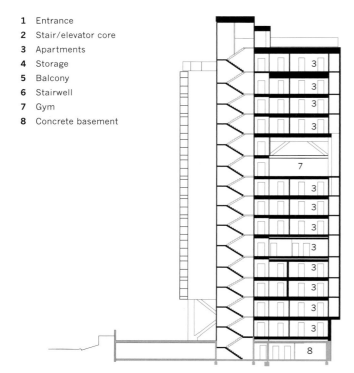

Section AA

performance of the otherwise lightweight building, making it less susceptible to large deflections or vibrations in strong wind conditions. At the same time, the 'power storey' supports the next four floors of apartment modules.

Preliminary cost estimates determined that a wood structure would be more expensive than the conventional steel or concrete alternatives. It was therefore decided to maximize the use of prefabrication to reduce construction time and so close the cost gap as far as possible. Typical apartment units in Treet consist of two volumetric modules, one 'wet', containing the kitchen and bathroom areas, and one 'dry', containing the living and bedroom spaces. The modules were manufactured in Estonia and shipped fully fitted out with windows, doors, cabinetry, plumbing fixtures, carpets, plasterboard and other finishes. The waterfront location in Bergen made the transfer of modules from ship to site efficient, with modules being lifted into place by crane.

On completion of the concrete plinth, erection of the building began with the placement of the apartment modules for the first four storeys. These modules carry their own weight and are set back from the exterior structure by a distance of 346mm. This is in part a construction tolerance, and in part a requirement to ensure the outer structure does not impact the modules when deflected by large wind loads.

Next the first 15 metre sections of the vertical trusses were anchored to the concrete and connected with diagonal braces. The first sections of the CLT elevator and stair cores were erected, followed by the lateral trusses for the 'power storey'. The fifth-floor modules

Treet under construction: View of single module, close-up of glulam structure surrounding modules, a crane is used to lift the modules into place.

Construction sequence

1 Construction modules are built up to four storeys. **2** The glulam structure is built around the modules. **3** The fifth-floor modules are inserted within the 'power deck' structure, and the concrete floor is cast to form a platform for the storeys above. Easy access to service allows for adaptability and reuse within the building. **4** Each five-storey segment is built in this fashion, with four storeys of modules supported by each 'power deck'.

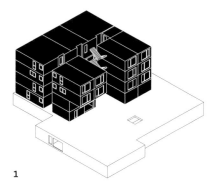

1

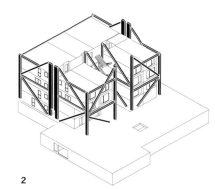

2

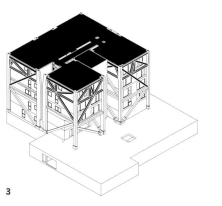

3

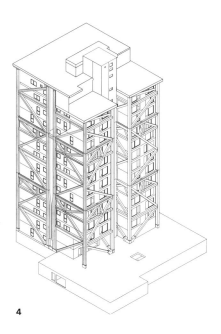

4

The glulam structure gives a unique character to this apartment interior.

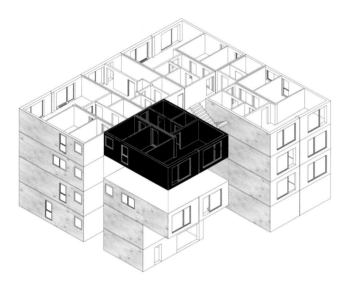

Diagram of modules

Each apartment is composed of a 'wet' and a 'dry' volumetric module that are first locked together and then locked in place. These modules are stacked four storeys high and then the glulam structure is built around them.

Detail section

1 3mm Corten sheets
2 48mm × 48mm battens
3 Laminated timber
4 Rockwool flex insulation
5 'Power deck' concrete floor
6 Ventilated cavity
7 Dimensional lumber
8 Membrane
9 Gypsum wallboard

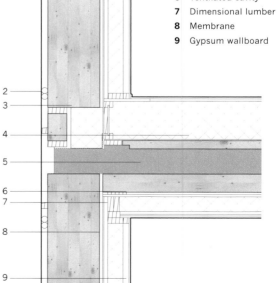

Many apartments feature elements of the exposed glulam structure and have views of Damsgardssundet beyond.

were then inserted between the trusses and connected to them (rather than resting on the modules below). Precast concrete slabs were subsequently laid on top of the trusses to form a base for the next four storeys. The process was then repeated for levels six through nine, and 11–14, with a 'power storey' again at level ten.

Enclosing the entire structure in metal and glass protects the wood from moisture and ultraviolet degradation, and also permits the glulams to be specified for interior rather than exterior use. The modules are designed to Passive House standard and, because each has its own floors, wall and ceiling assemblies, when the modules are placed together on site, there are two layers of construction both horizontally and vertically between units. This arrangement meets the required acoustic standards without any additional measures being necessary.

The fully exposed glulam structure is required to have a fire resistance of 90 minutes, and this is achieved by oversizing the members and calculating the charring

rate as described in chapter 5, Building Performance, pp. 41–42, in this book. Typical member sizes are 405mm × 650mm and 495mm × 495mm for the truss members, and 405mm × 405mm for the cross braces. All steel connections are concealed and protected by the wood. Exposed glulam and CLT surfaces were painted with a flame-retardant finish in the corridors and exit areas. To prevent the spread of fire, the cavity between the apartment modules and the exterior wall assembly is divided into compartments that follow the diagonal geometry of the trusses.

CONCLUSION

Treet is the result of a highly pragmatic approach to design that draws on tradition and local expertise in glulam fabrication to create a uniquely Norwegian structural solution. With the addition of CLT panels from Germany and Estonian apartment modules, the architecture is expressed as a mechanistic 'kit of parts' that repositions wood as an unequivocally modern construction material.

NEW VISIONS, NEW HEIGHTS

In the preceding chapters, we have profiled the completed works of more than 50 architectural and structural engineering firms from 11 different countries who, together with their clients, must be considered the true pioneers of Tall Wood architecture. Working behind the scenes are wood industry researchers and building code consultants who have helped address some of the perceptual barriers and technical challenges that must be faced when designing a Tall Wood building.

Whether the result is a five-storey structure, or a 15-storey tower, each project has addressed the legislative requirements of fire and life safety and the physical considerations of movement control and moisture protection. Collectively these projects have advanced our understanding of what is possible using this new

technology, and opened the door to a new era of environmentally sustainable building practice.

However, this is just the beginning. Tall Wood has begun to attract the attention of the mainstream media, and momentum continues to grow with the announcement of each new project. Some of these projects are fully funded, approved and ready to break ground; others are competition-winning entries or aspirational designs by architects and structural engineers eager to enter the Tall Wood arena with their own 'proof of concept' proposals. Following are descriptions of several of these projects, presented in alphabetical order.

475 WEST 18TH, NEW YORK, USA

Designed by SHoP Architects, this project was one of two winners in the US Tall Wood Building Prize Com-

Brock Commons. The student residence, designed by Acton Ostry and Hermann Kaufmann, rises 18 stories over the University of British Columbia Campus, 17 stories of wood construction sit atop a concrete base.

The wood structure was designed so that floor, wall and column components could be prefabricated off site, then shipped when needed. This minimized on-site storage and reduced overall construction time compared with traditional methods of project delivery.

petition announced in September 2015. The competition, sponsored by the US Department of Agriculture in partnership with the Softwood Lumber Board and the Binational Softwood Lumber Council, awarded a total of $3 million in prize money to support projects that could advance the understanding and acceptance of Tall Wood buildings throughout the USA.

A ten-storey residential condominium in Manhattan's West Chelsea neighbourhood, 475 West 18th Street, is located immediately opposite the iconic High Line Park. The project will contain 15 two-, three-, and four-bedroom apartments. The building will be the first in New York City to use modern massive wood systems, and will be the tallest building in the city to use structural timber, pending approvals from the New York City Department of Buildings.

To celebrate the unique nature of the project, the engineered wood structure will be exposed wherever functionally appropriate and permitted by code. In addition to that, other wood materials and finishes will be used throughout the building to maximize the environmental benefits of carbon sequestration and substitution. This will be part of a broad sustainability strategy designed to minimize the impact of building construction and operations. The project will target LEED Platinum certification, but also pursue higher levels of sustainability not captured by the LEED program.

BROCK COMMONS, VANCOUVER, CANADA

In November 2015, construction began on the 18-storey Brock Commons student residence at the University of British Columbia in Vancouver. Designed by Acton Ostry Architects and Architekten Hermann Kaufmann, the building will provide housing for 404

students with a mix of studio and quad units, as well as social and study amenity spaces.

The structure is a hybrid system comprised of CLT floor slabs, glulam columns, steel connectors and concrete cores. When completed in 2017, Brock Commons will stand 53 metres tall. The building will connect to the UBC District Energy System and has been designed to target LEED Gold certification.

FRAMEWORK, PORTLAND, USA

The second winner in the US Tall Wood Building Prize Competition, Framework is a 12-storey mixed-use building proposed by Lever Architecture for Portland, Oregon. The grant will be used to fund research to determine the viability of CLT and other engineered wood products in high-rise construction in the United States. This will include working with code, fire and other authorities to ensure that current concerns can be addressed and regulatory compliance achieved. The building will consist of one level of ground floor retail, five levels of office, five levels of workforce housing and a rooftop amenity space. With a prominent location and high public visibility, the building is designed with a transparent glazed façade to better communicate its innovative use of wood products and construction technology at street level.

HARBOURSIDE, NORTH VANCOUVER, CANADA

Harbourside is a 93,000 square metre mixed-use development to be located on the waterfront in North Vancouver, British Columbia. Designed by MGA | Michael Green Architecture, Harbourside will be constructed entirely of wood from the ground up. The program is 80% residential and 20% commercial,

HSBC Competition Tower. C.F. Møller's proposal for a 34-storey housing complex aims to bring Tall Wood buildings to the heart of Stockholm, Sweden.

with the tallest buildings reaching 11 storeys – the maximum height currently permitted by the official community plan.

The structures will be a combination of load-bearing CLT and glulam post-and-beam construction, with CLT elevator and stair cores. The project has the backing of a private developer, and construction is scheduled to start in 2017. In scope and scale Harbourside has the potential to transform the way North America thinks about massive wood construction.

HOHO, VIENNA, AUSTRIA

Designed by Arch. Rüdiger Lainer, the proposal for HoHo Wien, a 24-storey commercial building containing a hotel, offices and wellness centre, was announced in March of 2015. The project combines wood and concrete in a hybrid construction designed to optimize the use of wood components and systems already available on the market, with a concrete podium, stair and elevator shafts that address the fire protection requirements of the Vienna building code. Wood composite floors are secured to the central concrete supporting cores, and extend out to the building

edge. These floor panels are supported by a wooden column system around the perimeter of the building. This structure then supports prefabricated external wall modules that combine solid wood panels with an earth-tone concrete. The timber construction combines durability with good thermal performance. Design calculations indicate that in total, approximately 75% of the material used in the 84 metre tall structure will be wood.

HSBC COMPETITION TOWER, STOCKHOLM, SWEDEN

This 34-storey residential tower is one of three shortlisted proposals in a competition organized in 2013 by HSBC, Sweden's largest building society. The intent of the competition was to explore housing solutions that could be realized using current and emerging technologies and completed by 2023, HSBC's centennial year. Designed by C.F. Møller, the project includes a ground floor cafe, childcare centre, and a glazed community garden for use by residents, as well as a publicly accessible market square, fitness facility and community centre. As proposed, the building has a central con-

Harbourside. This proposal for a mixed-use development by MGA | Michael Green Architecture would set a North American precedent in terms of scale and scope.

Loudden Harbour Development. This proposal by Tham & Videgård will be a major component in the redevelopment of this former commercial port in Stockholm, Sweden.

HoHo Wien. The 24-storey HoHo development in Vienna by Arch. Rüdiger Lainer will introduce a new Tall Wood typology to the Austrian capital.

crete service core, although this could be built in wood if acceptable to the regulatory authorities at the time of construction. Whatever the choice of material, the surrounding post-and-beam structure will be exposed internally, and visible from the outside, both through the windows and through the glazed balconies that are a feature of each apartment.

HYPÉRION HOUSING AND OFFICE COMPLEX, BORDEAUX, FRANCE

This competition-winning proposal by French architect Jean-Paul Viguier is notable for its integration of structure and nature. The Hypérion development will include 17,000 square metres of residential and office space in three towers with engineered wood structures. The central residential tower is 18 storeys (57 metres) in height and covered with plant-filled balconies. The building will contain five or six apartments per floor, with duplex units at roof level.

To either side are a nine-storey housing block with integrated parking, and a seven-storey office block formed from prefabricated boxes stacked one on top of the other. The central tower will have a concrete core, but the flanking buildings will be all wood – a combination of glulam post-and-beam structure with CLT floors and walls. Work on Hypérion is expected to begin in late 2017 and be completed in 2020.

LOUDDEN HARBOUR DEVELOPMENT, STOCKHOLM, SWEDEN

This proposal by architects Tham & Videgård for a 24,700 square metre mixed-use project on the Stockholm waterfront was commissioned by Folkhem (developer of Strandparken Hus B) as part of a wider regeneration of Loudden Harbour, a former industrial area on the island of Djurgården.

The four residential towers will be constructed entirely of Swedish pine, including the structural components, façade, finishes and windows. The towers will be connected by a three-storey base and will collectively provide 240 new homes for the city, as well as quayside restaurants, cafes and indoor gardens.

OAKWOOD TOWER, LONDON, ENGLAND

If realized, this 300 metre tall tower would be London's second tallest building and its first wooden skyscraper. Conceived by PLP Architecture in collaboration with a research team from the University of Cambridge, the 80-storey residential tower is proposed as an addition to the Barbican Housing estate. With a floor area of 93,000 square metres, the building could accommodate up to 1000 apartments. Structural engineers Smith and Wallwork performed a comparative analysis of a number of different frame concepts using massive timber elements that would require some 65,000 cubic metres of engineered timber. The final design utilized a buttressed mega-truss solution with 2.5 × 2.5 metre timber columns and 1.75 metre thick timber walls. Despite using significant volumes of timber the structure would be four times lighter than a concrete equivalent.

CONCLUSION

The Tall Wood projects included here, and others currently being imagined, speak to the ever-increasing breadth and depth of knowledge and experience that is being amassed by the design and construction industry worldwide. A century ago, a similar momentum was building around the construction of concrete and steel skyscrapers in Chicago and New York. What characterized that era was a spirit of healthy competition that accelerated the development of high-rise technology at an unprecedented rate. Now, on a global scale, a similar pattern is emerging, as a growing number of countries embrace Tall Wood construction, not simply as a matter of bragging rights, but as a holistic approach to the environmental crisis we face, and as a sustainable means to support economic and social development on an international scale.

GLOSSARY OF TERMS AND ACRONYMS

Bending A force applied to a structural member that causes it to adopt a curved shape. The inside face of the curve will experience compression, while the outside face will be subjected to tension.

Billet The extruded form in which an engineered wood product is produced. It may be a square section (as with parallel strand lumber) or a flat panel (as with laminated strand lumber).

Castellated Having a profile of alternating projections and incisions, as with the battlements of a castle.

Compression Opposing forces applied in the same axis but in opposing directions that cause a material to shorten in length or width.

CLT – cross-laminated timber CLT is an engineered wood product in which layers of small section timber form a panel product that can be used for floors, walls or roofs. The orientation of grain in any given layer is perpendicular to that of the adjacent layers, giving CLT two-way spanning capability.

CNC – computerized numerical control The system by which machines can be programmed to cut, plane and rout timber elements using instructions from a three-dimensional digital model.

Dead load A load within a building that is fixed in magnitude, direction and position, as with the weight of the structure itself.

Diaphragm action The ability of a planar element (e.g. a wall, floor or roof) to transfer loads both parallel and perpendicular to its edges without permanent deformation.

EBD – environmental building declaration A document published by Athena Sustainable Materials Institute in Ottawa that tabulates and quantifies a standard set of environmental impacts associated with the construction and operation of a building. It is sometimes seen as analogous to a nutrition label on a food package.

EMC – equilibrium moisture content The point at which the percentage moisture content in a piece of wood is equal to the moisture content of the environment in which it is installed. Typically the EMC will be between 8–12% (varying with season) in a conditioned building.

EWP – engineered wood product A manufactured material in which small wood pieces, veneers or wood fibres are combined through mechanical processing and chemical bonding, to form a composite material with superior properties to those of natural wood.

Fire separation A separation between adjacent spaces or compartments in a building that, by way of prior testing, will resist the passage of fire from one side to the other for a prescribed period of time.

Furring strips Small dimension wood sections (typically 25mm × 50mm) used to create an air space between a finish material such as gypsum wallboard, and the substrate to which it is being fastened.

GHG – greenhouse gas A gas that occurs naturally or is released into the atmosphere, that is transparent to incident solar radiation, yet opaque to reflected heat from the Earth's surface, therefore causing heat to build up in the atmosphere. The most common GHG is carbon dioxide (CO_2) and one of the most powerful is methane (CH4).

GLT – glue laminated timber An engineered wood panel product made up from glued laminated sections of solid sawn wood.

Header A short beam of wood or other material used to span an opening and transfer the vertical loads to which it is subjected, to the supporting walls or posts on either side.

Hold-down anchor A hardware device designed to resist the uplift forces to which a building may be subjected during wind or seismic events. Typically the anchor is embedded in a concrete foundation or substructure. It may take the form of a bracket, or may be a continuous rod that extends the full height of the building.

HSS – hollow square section A standard structural steel profile that has four sides of equal dimension, encasing a void.

Hygroscopic The property of wood that makes it able to absorb moisture from the air.

IIC – impact insulation class A North American measure of the ability of a floor/ceiling or wall element to attenuate the transmission of sound from a physical impact such as a foot fall. The scale is logarithmic, i.e. the higher the IIC number, the greater the attenuation of sound. The measurement method is similar to that used in Europe for the equivalent rating (known as impact sound insulation or ISI) although actual values may differ slightly.

Interstitial condensation The precipitation of liquid water that occurs within the structure of an exterior wall or roof. This precipitation occurs when the temperature of a surface is too low to sustain the amount of water vapour carried by the air touching it.

ISI – impact sound insulation A European measure of the ability of a floor/ceiling or wall element to attenuate the transmission of sound from a physical impact such as a foot fall. The scale is logarithmic – the higher the ISI number, the greater the attenuation of sound. The measurement method is similar to that used in North America for the equivalent rating (known as impact insulation class or IIC) although actual values may differ slightly.

Lag screw A heavy wood screw with a square or hexagonal head.

Lap joint A joint made with two panels or planks of wood, by halving the thickness of each piece at the joint and fitting them together in an overlapping configuration.

Lateral resistance The ability of structure to resist horizontal forces applied to it, most often by wind or seismic activity.

LCA – life cycle assessment An internationally recognized objective methodology that assesses the environmental impacts of a material, product, assembly or whole building, from extraction through fabrication, installation, building operations and end of life disposal. A whole building LCA is sometimes referred to as an > environmental building declaration (EBD).

Lintel A beam of wood or other material used to span a door or window opening and transfer the vertical loads to which it is subjected on to the supporting walls or posts on either side.

Live load Any fluctuating or intermittent load to which a building may be subjected. The load may be internal (as with occupants or furniture) or external (as with wind or snow loads).

LSL – laminated strand lumber An > engineered wood product made from elongated strands or flakes of wood fibre, bonded together with glue and pressed into panel form.

LVL – laminated veneer lumber An > engineered wood product in which long strips of veneer are glued face to face in a vertical orientation to form a panel.

Load path The sequence of structural elements in a building through which dead and live loads are transmitted to the ground. These elements may be horizontal (as roofs, floors or beams), vertical (as walls or posts), or diagonal (as the elements of a truss).

Massive timber Often used in its short version 'mass timber', the term was first applied to > cross-laminated timber (CLT) panel construction in which both vertical and horizontal structural elements were of solid CLT. In this book, it is used to describe construction in which the dimensions of all structural elements, whether posts, beams or panels are large enough to perform predictably when exposed to fire. In this way, mass timber is different from traditional light frame construction.

MC – moisture content Moisture content is the ratio of the mass of water in a piece of wood to the mass of the wood when dry, expressed as a percentage.

NLT –nail laminated timber A prefabricated wood product in which solid sawn members are mechanically fastened (with nails or screws) face to face, to create a solid panel most often used for floors or roofs.

OSB – oriented strand board An > engineered wood product in which elongated flakes of wood fibre are glued together under pressure to form a panel, most typically used for sheathing or decking as an alternative to plywood.

PEFC – Program for the Endorsement of Forest Certification Schemes A Swiss-based not for profit organization that certifies national and regional forest management standards against an agreed set of environmental criteria.

PSL – parallel strand lumber A proprietary > engineered wood product in which elongated strands of wood fibre are glued together under pressure to form a billet that is square in section. Typically cut into standard lumber sizes, PSL is most often used for posts, beams and lintels.

Progressive collapse Most often used in relation to high-rise buildings, progressive collapse is the phenomenon by which the failure in the structure of an upper floor adds to the load on the floor below it, causing that floor (and successive lower floors) to collapse.

Scarf joint A joint connecting two pieces of wood in which the ends are beveled or notched so that they fit over or into each other.

Self-tapping screw A screw that can tap or drill its own hole as it is driven into a piece of wood. Such screws generally have a fluted point that acts in much the same way as a drill bit.

Shear A force exerted when two opposing forces are offset slightly from one another – as with the blades of a pair of scissors.

Shear bracket A connection device that increases the ability of a wood member or assembly to resist shear forces.

Slip joint A joint designed to accommodate differential movement between two adjacent elements of a structure, while maintaining the integrity of the assembly. For example, a connection at the top of a (non-load-bearing) curtain wall may include a slip joint to accommodate deflection of the roof under snow load, while maintaining the ability of the curtain wall to resist horizontal wind loads.

Spline A type of connection in which two boards or panels are fitted with matching grooves along their meeting edges, and both are filled with a single thin strip of wood (known as a spline).

SFM – sustainable forest management A system of third party administered forest management practices and protocols (including reforestation) that ensure that the harvesting of wood from a given forest does not compromise the ecological services provided by that forest, nor deplete its overall stock of wood fibre over time.

SRI – Sound Reduction Index In Europe the Sound Reduction Index is used to measure the level of airborne sound insulation provided by a structure such as a wall, window or door. The unit of measurement is the decibel; the higher the SRI, the greater the level of sound insulation provided.

STC – Sound Transmission Class In North America, the Sound Transmission Class is used to measure the level of airborne sound insulation provided by a structure such as a wall, window or door. The unit of measurement is the decibel; the higher the STC, the greater the level of sound insulation provided.

Tension Opposing forces applied in the same axis but in opposing directions, that cause a material to increase in length or width.

Thermal conductivity The rate at which heat passes through a specified material, expressed as the amount of heat that flows per unit time through a unit area with a temperature gradient of one degree per unit distance.

Thermal mass The ability of a material to absorb and store heat energy.

Torsion The twisting of a structural element due to the application of a force or forces that cause one end of a beam, column or panel element to rotate relative to the other end.

UNFAO – United Nations Food and Agriculture Organization UNFAO is an agency of the United Nations that leads international efforts to defeat hunger. Serving both developed and developing countries, UNFAO acts as a neutral forum where all nations meet as equals to negotiate agreements and debate policy.

VOC – volatile organic compound In reference to the paints, coatings, bonding agents and other compounds used in building materials and products, VOCs include many carbon-based compounds that participate in atmospheric chemical reactions, characterized by the evaporation or 'outgassing' that is part of the curing process.

ABOUT THE AUTHORS

MICHAEL GREEN

Michael founded his architecture firm MGA | Michael Green Architecture and his not for profit school DBR | Design Build Research to focus on progressive architecture, research, education and innovation. From offices in Vancouver and Portland, he and his team work on international projects that are diverse in their scale, building type and location.

Michael is vested in helping build healthier communities through innovative architecture, interiors, landscape and urban design. Michael is particularly known for his research, leadership and advocacy in promoting the use of wood in the built environment with extensive international talks on the subject, including his 2013 TED talk which has been viewed over a million times.

ANDREW WAUGH

Andrew Waugh founded Waugh Thistleton Architects in 2000 in Shoreditch, London. Andrew was a pioneer in the architectural quest for Tall Wood buildings with Waugh Thistleton's nine-storey timber Murray Grove project in London in 2009. Waugh Thistleton continue to build internationally in timber, with high-profile projects such as Dalston Lane in Hackney, London. This apartment complex is scheduled for completion in 2017 and will be the world's largest CLT structure.

JIM TAGGART

Since leaving architectural practice in 1992, Jim has written and lectured extensively on the use of wood in contemporary architecture to audiences throughout North America and across the world. He is also the author of the award-winning book *Toward a Culture of Wood Architecture* (2011).

Jim has taught architecture at the British Columbia Institute of Technology in Vancouver since 2004, and has been editor of *Sustainable Architecture and Building Magazine* (SABMag) since its inception in 2006. He is a Fellow of the Royal Architectural Institute of Canada, a Director of the Athena Sustainable Materials Institute and was the recipient of the 2012 Premier of British Columbia's 'Wood Champion' award.

ACKNOWLEDGMENTS

We would like to thank our families, friends, the office of MGA | Michael Green Architecture and Design Build Research (DBR) for being a constant source of motivation, inspiration and support; and our students and fellow practitioners whose eagerness to embrace the Tall Wood movement adds momentum to our search for a more environmentally responsible and socially just architecture.

We would also like to thank all the architects, contractors, building owners and professionals who contributed to the development of this book, and who continue to advance the theory and practice of Tall Wood building across the world. In particular, a special thanks to Andrew Waugh, a true Tall Wood pioneer, who contributed the foreword, and to our technical advisors:

Chapters 4 Structural Systems and 7 Technology
Eric Karsh, Principal
Equilibrium Consulting Inc., Vancouver, Canada

Chapter 5 Building Performance

Fire Safety
Geoff Triggs, Principal
Evolution Building Science Ltd., Vancouver, Canada

Acoustic Performance
Tim Preager, Principal
Aercoustics Engineering Ltd., Toronto, Canada

Thermal Performance
Graham Finch, Principal
RDH Building Science Inc., Vancouver, Canada

In addition we would like to extend our personal thanks to those individuals who contributed to the research and production of material:

MGA design and production team lead
Stuart Lodge

MGA team members
Kyla Leslie, Monika E. Löfvenmark, Dawn Melody, Harry Olson, Amanda Reed

BCIT student research team
Jordi Ashworth, Anthony Chen, Justin Deddens, Nicholas Dellai, Jivan Khera, Luca Luca Alessi, Michael Nguyen, Kim Scharf, Navjot Singh, Gloria Wu, Daria Zubkova

Michael Green and Jim Taggart

INDEX OF BUILDINGS, NAMES AND LOCATIONS

ILLUSTRATION CREDITS

Cover photograph Ed White; **8** Michael Green; **10** Asher DeGroot; **12** Michael Green; **14, 15** Food and Agriculture Organization of the United Nations/MGA | Michael Green Architecture; **16** MGA | Michael Green Architecture; **17 left** Laurent Coulard; **17 right** Emma Cross; **18** Food and Agriculture Organization of the United Nations/MGA | Michael Green Architecture; **20** W. J. Moore, City of Vancouver Archives; **23–24** MGA | Michael Green Architecture; **24 left** Ole Jais; **24 right** Will Pryce; **25** MGA | Michael Green Architecture; **27** MGA | Michael Green Architecture; **28** MGA | Michael Green Architecture; **31** MGA | Michael Green Architecture; **32** Leonard Frank, City of Vancouver Archives; **34** Gilles Huot; **35** Brad Kahn; **36** MGA | Michael Green Architecture; **37 top** Bruno Klomfar; **37 bottom** Schluder Architecture/MGA | Michael Green Architecture; **38 left** Brend Borchardt; **38 right** Tim Crocker; **39** Stuart Thomson, City of Vancouver Archives; **42** Lendlease; **43** Ed White; **44** Martin Tessler; **45** MGA | Michael Green Architecture; **49** Wesley Wollin; **52** Major J. S. Matthews, City of Vancouver Archives; **54** Oskar Leo Kaufmann; **55** Adolf Bereuter; **56** Richard Osbourne; **58** Jack Lindsay, City of Vancouver Archives; **60** MGA | Michael Green Architecture; **61 left** Shigeru Ban Architects; **61 right** Paul Alberts/Forestry Innovation Investment; **63** MGA | Michael Green Architecture; **64, 65** Ioana Marinescu; **66** Karakusevic Carson Architects/MGA | Michael Green Architecture; **67 top** Karakusevic Carson Architects; **67 bottom** MGA | Michael Green Architecture; **68** Karakusevic Carson Architects; **69** Karakusevic Carson Architects/MGA | Michael Green Architecture; **70** Tord-Rikard Söderström; **71 left** Wingårdh Arkitektkontor/MGA | Michael Green Architecture; **71 right** Tord-Rikard Söderström; **72 left** Wingårdh Arkitektkontor/MGA | Michael Green Architecture (drawings); **72 right top** Wingårdh Arkitektkontor (photograph); **72 right bottom** Johan Ardefors (photograph); **73** MGA | Michael Green Architecture; **74** Tord-Rikard Söderström; **75** Wingårdh Arkitektkontor/MGA | Michael Green Architecture; **76** Pietro Savorelli; **77 top** Rossiprodi Associati/MGA | Michael Green Architecture; **77 bottom** Pietro Savorelli; **78 top** Rossiprodi Associati/MGA | Michael Green Architecture; **79** Acrangelo Del Piai; **80** MGA | Michael Green Architecture; **81** Pietro Savorelli; **82, 83, 84 top** Martin Kunze; **84 bottom** Architekturagentur Stuttgart/MGA | Michael Green Architecture; **85 top** Bernadette Grimmenstein; **85 bottom** Architekturagentur Stuttgart/MGA | Michael Green Architecture; **86 top** Martin Kunze (photographs); **86 bottom** MGA | Michael Green Architecture (drawing); **87, 88 top** Martin Kunze (photographs); **88 bottom** MGA | Michael Green Architecture (drawing); **89** Martin Kunze; **90** MGA | Michael Green Architecture; **91** Architekturagentur Stuttgart/MGA | Michael Green Architecture; **92** Martin Kunze; **94** Mikko Auerniitty; **95 left** OOPEAA/MGA | Michael Green Architecture; **95 right** Mikko Auerniitty; **96** OOPEAA/MGA | Michael Green Architecture; **97 top** Mikko Auerniitty (photographs); **97 bottom** OOPEAA/MGA | Michael Green Architecture; **98 top** Jurha Pakkala; **98 bottom** MGA | Michael Green Architecture; **99** Mikko Auerniitty; **101** MGA | Michael Green Architecture; **102** Martin Tessler; **103** Latreille Delage Photography; **104** Perkins + Will/MGA | Michael Green Architecture; **105 top** John Boys (photographs); **105 bottom** MGA | Michael Green Architecture; **106 top** MGA | Michael Green Architecture (drawings); **106 bottom** John Boys (photographs); **107 left** Latreille Delage Photography; **107 right** Martin Tessler; **108, 109** Didier Boy de la Tour; **110, 111** Shigeru Ban Architects/MGA | Michael Green Architecture; **112** Shigeru Ban Architects; **113** Shigeru Ban Architects/MGA | Michael Green Architecture; **114 top** Shigeru Ban Architects (photographs); **114 bottom** MGA | Michael Green Architecture (drawings); **115** Shigeru Ban Architects (photographs); **115 bottom** MGA | Michael Green Architecture (drawings); **116** Shigeru Ban Architects/MGA | Michael Green Architecture; **117** Didier Boy de la Tour; **118** Brad Kahn; **119 left** The Miller Hull Partnership/MGA | Michael Green Architecture (drawing); **119 right** Brad Kahn (photographs);

120 The Miller Hull Partnership/MGA | Michael Green Architecture; **121** Brad Kahn; **122 left** MGA | Michael Green Architecture (drawings); **122** John Stamets (photographs); **123** Brad Kahn; **124** Ema Peter; **125** Ed White; **126** MGA | Michael Green Architecture; **127** Ema Peter; **128 top** MGA | Michael Green Architecture (drawings); **128 bottom** Paul Alberts/Forestry Innovation Investment (photographs); **129 top** MGA | Michael Green Architecture (drawings); **129 bottom** Paul Alberts/Forestry Innovation Investment (photographs); **130** MGA | Michael Green Architecture; **131 top** MGA | Michael Green Architecture; **131 bottom, 132, 133** Ema Peter; **135** MGA | Michael Green Architecture; **136** Giuseppe Micciché; **137, 138** Pool Architekten/MGA | Michael Green Architecture; **139 top left** Giuseppe Micciché; **139 top right** Pool Architekten; **139 bottom** Pool Architekten/MGA | Michael Green Architecture; **140** Giuseppe Micciché; **141 top** MGA | Michael Green Architecture; **141 bottom** Pool Architekten; **142, 143, 144 top** RADON photography/Norman Radon; **144 bottom, 145** Architekten Hermann Kaufmann/MGA | Michael Green Architecture; **146 top** MGA | Michael Green Architecture (drawing); **146 bottom** Norman A. Müller (photographs); **147 top** MGA | Michael Green Architecture; **147 bottom** Architekten Hermann Kaufmann/MGA | Michael Green Architecture; **148 bottom** Norman A. Müller (photographs); **148 right** MGA | Michael Green Architecture (drawing); **149 top** Architekten Hermann Kaufmann (photographs); **149 bottom** MGA | Michael Green Architecture (drawing); **150, 151** RADON photography/Norman Radon; **152, 153 left** Jack Hobhouse; **153 right, 154 top** Hawkins\Brown/MGA | Michael Green Architecture (drawings); **154 bottom** Norman A. Müller; **155** Norman A. Müller; **156** MGA | Michael Green Architecture; **157 top** Norman A. Müller (photographs); **157 bottom** Hawkins\Brown/MGA | Michael Green Architecture (drawing); **158** Marina Trifkovic; **159** MGA | Michael Green Architecture; **160** Artec Arkitekter/MGA | Michael Green Architecture; **161 top** Artec Arkitekter/MGA | Michael Green Architecture (photographs); **161 bottom** MGA | Michael Green Architecture (drawings); **162 top** Morten Pedersen, Inviso; **162 middle** MGA | Michael Green Architecture; **162 bottom** Artec Arkitekter/MGA | Michael Green Architecture; **163** Morten Pedersen, Inviso; **164** MGA | Michael Green Architecture; **165** Seagate Structures; **166** C. F. Møller; **167** MGA | Michael Green Architecture; **168 top** Tham & Videgård; **168 bottom** Arch. Rüdiger Lainer;

Every reasonable attempt has been made to identify owners of copyright. If unintentional mistakes or omissions occurred, we sincerely apologize and ask for notice. Such mistakes will be corrected in the next edition of this publication.